My Queen,
My Mother

"Marge Steinhage Fenelon brings the reader on a pilgrimage to shrines of our Lady in the United States, journeying through the terrain of our country and the landscape of our own hearts. Both historical and personal, *My Queen, My Mother* reminds us to depend even more on the loving mother who wants to continue to shape our country and our lives."

Fr. Michael Gaitley, MIC
Author of *33 Days to Morning Glory*

"This beautifully written book shows how Marian shrines are special places of encounter with our merciful Mother, who leads us toward her divine Son, Jesus."

Robert Fastiggi
Professor of systematic theology at Sacred Heart Major Seminary
Former president of the Mariological Society of America

"While on our pilgrimage to the kingdom of heaven, there are many places for us to stop and pray here on earth. Marge Steinhage Fenelon serves as your tour guide and pilgrimage coordinator for your armchair pilgrimage. At each US shrine you will meet your heavenly mother who invites you into her home, loves you, prays for you daily, and invites you to love her as your mother. Let this book be the beginning or deepening of your love for Mary."

Rev. Edward Looney
Author of *A Heart Like Mary's*

"Marge Steinhage Fenelon teaches us to be pilgrims through life and to stay close to Blessed Mother Mary, who always leads us to her Son."

Donna-Marie Cooper O'Boyle
Catholic author, international speaker, and EWTN host

"As a lifelong pilgrim who has known the joy and power of journeys to sacred sites, I'm thrilled to have the opportunity to learn from and pray with gifted author Marge Steinhage Fenelon. With *My Queen, My Mother*, Fenelon invites us along for a life-changing encounter to know our Lord through the heart and soul of his most devoted disciple, his mother. Prepare to be inspired, challenged, and sent on a lifelong mission of devotion and love!"

Lisa M. Hendey
Author of *The Grace of Yes*

My Queen, My Mother

A LIVING NOVENA

A MARIAN PILGRIMAGE ACROSS AMERICA

Marge Steinhage Fenelon

AVE MARIA PRESS AVE Notre Dame, Indiana

© 2019 by Marge Fenelon

All rights reserved. No part of this book may be used or reproduced in any manner whatsoever, except in the case of reprints in the context of reviews, without written permission from Ave Maria Press®, Inc., P.O. Box 428, Notre Dame, IN 46556, 1-800-282-1865.

Founded in 1865, Ave Maria Press is a ministry of the United States Province of Holy Cross.

www.avemariapress.com

Paperback: ISBN-13 978-1-59471-815-1

E-book: ISBN-13 978-1-59471-816-8

Cover art by Rose Walton.

Stock Images by gettyimages.com, vecteezy.com.

Cover and text design by Katherine Robinson.

Printed and bound in the United States of America.

Library of Congress Cataloging-in-Publication Data is available.

To my father,

George Steinhage,

from whom I inherited my wanderlust

and insatiable love for history.

Contents

Directory of Marian Shrines

For more information about the Marian shrines explored in this book, visit these websites.

Shrine of Our Lady of La Leche
https://missionandshrine.org

National Shrine of Our Lady of Prompt Succor
https://www.shrineofourladyofpromptsuccor.com

St. Mary's Mission and Museum
http://www.saintmarysmission.org

Shrine of Our Lady of Sorrows
http://vivaro-hshrine-primary.cluster2.hgsitebuilder.com

Basilica and National Shrine of Our Lady of Consolation
https://www.olcshrine.com

The National Shrine of Our Lady of Good Help
https://www.shrineofourladyofgoodhelp.com

Shrine of Our Lady of Martyrs
http://www.auriesvilleshrine.com

The House of Mary Shrine
https://sites.google.com/view/
the-house-of-mary-shrine/home

Our Lady of Peace Shrine
http://www.olop-shrine.org

Refugium Peccatorum Madonna, Luigi Crosio, 1898. Commonly known as "Mother Thrice Admirable."

Introduction

WHY A MARIAN PILGRIMAGE?

As I made my way on my Marian pilgrimage, I was most often asked one question: "Why are you doing this?"

The idea started percolating in my brain as I watched the growing success of my book *Our Lady, Undoer of Knots: A Living Novena*. It seems that the notion of taking my reader on pilgrimage with me and then forming it into a novena had become contagious. I wanted to do it again, but this time I wanted to stay within my own country's boundaries. I wanted to do something challenging and magnificent that would uncover the spiritual treasures of our United States and, in the process, help people to fall in love with our country again (or perhaps for the first time). Recent history has seen our nation in the throes of hostile divisions, skepticism, and an encroaching godlessness. The early missionaries came to this continent to conquer it for Christ, and many of the places they founded were dedicated to Mary. I wanted to reconquer it

for our Lord and his Mother and help others to set
out to reconquer it too.

The best way to reconquer anything is to first
reconquer it spiritually. I know many people who
go to great lengths to travel on pilgrimage to distant places—the Holy Land, of course, but also
Marian places such as Lourdes, France; Fatima,
Portugal; and Knock, Ireland, to name a few. They
make painstaking plans and invest their time,
energy, and money into the journey. More than
anything, they invest their spirits by preparing
mentally and spiritually beforehand so that they
can make a fruitful pilgrimage. I don't know anyone who has gone on pilgrimage and regretted it.
Nor do I know anyone who did not gain far more
than he or she invested.

What is a pilgrimage, really?

A pilgrimage is a holy journey to a sacred
destination, the purpose of which is to atone for
one's sins, live a spiritual experience, or implore
a particular grace, intention, or miracle with the
ultimate goal of drawing closer to God. Therefore,
pilgrimages should "cost" something in terms of
self-imposed hardships, such as fasting, almsgiv-
ing, simplicity, or the difficulty of the chosen route.

The custom of making pilgrimages dates
back to Old Testament times. After the building

of the First Temple in Jerusalem (ca. 957 BC), all
Jewish men were required to go to the Temple for
three major feasts: *Pesach* (the Feast of Unleavened
Bread, or Passover), *Shavu'ot* (the Feast of Weeks,
or Pentecost), and *Sukkot* (the Feast of Tabernacles,
or Festival of Ingathering). As they traveled, they
sang pilgrim songs (also called "songs of assent"
or "gradual canticles") that were derived from the
Psalms.[1] Consider also Abraham's pilgrimage as
described in the letter to the Hebrews: "By faith
Abraham obeyed when he was called to set out
for a place that he was to receive as an inheritance;
and he set out, not knowing where he was going.
By faith he stayed for a time in the land he had
been promised, as in a foreign land, living in tents,
as did Isaac and Jacob, who were heirs with him
of the same promise. For he looked forward to
the city that has foundations, whose architect and
builder is God" (11:8–10). Indeed, our Lord's entire
ministry narrative from the time of his baptism in
the Jordan to his Crucifixion in Jerusalem unfolds
as a pilgrimage.

Pilgrimages as we know them today became
popular after Christianity was legalized in the
Roman Empire in AD 313, as Christians yearned
to experience the Holy Land. Around the elev-
enth century, indulgences were intertwined with

pilgrimages, increasing their popularity. One of the most well-known pilgrimage destinations is the Cathedral of Santiago de Compostela in present-day Galicia, Spain. In AD 40, Mary appeared in the flesh to the apostle James, instructing him to build a church there in her honor, which he did. When she appeared, Mary was standing on a pillar made of jasper carried by angels. Before departing, she gave the pillar and a statue of herself holding Jesus to St. James, and he placed them in the church. Mary also instructed St. James to return to Jerusalem, where he would eventually suffer martyrdom. Since the ninth century, pilgrims have traveled the arduous path—known as El Camino de Santiago de Compostela—from El Salvador Cathedral in Oviedo, Spain, to Santiago de Compostela in Galicia, Spain. Nearly 300,000 pilgrims make the journey annually, walking the 200 miles of rough, rocky trails and staying in often primitive lodgings along the way.[2]

Why do the pilgrims put themselves through such hardship?

The Church advocates pilgrimages as a means for advancing in spiritual maturity. "Pilgrimages evoke our earthly journey toward heaven and are traditionally very special occasions for renewal in prayer. For pilgrims seeking living water, shrines are special places for living the forms of Christian prayer" (*CCC*, 2691).

Pope Benedict XVI pilgrimaged to the Cathedral of Santiago de Compostela in 2010. In his opening address, he said,

> To go on pilgrimage is not simply to visit a place to admire its treasures of nature, art or history. To go on pilgrimage really means to step out of ourselves in order to encounter God where he has revealed himself, where his grace has shone with particular splendor and produced rich fruits of conversion and holiness among those who believe. Above all, Christians go on pilgrimage to the Holy Land, to the places associated with the Lord's passion, death and resurrection. They go to Rome, the city of the martyrdom of Peter and Paul, and also to Compostela, which, associated with the memory of Saint James, has welcomed pilgrims from throughout the world who desire to strengthen their spirit with the Apostle's witness of faith and love.[3]

Pope Benedict XVI explained it perfectly—people go on pilgrimage in order to step out of themselves and into an encounter with God. A pilgrim seeks conversion and holiness, and those come at the price of striving and sacrifice. On pilgrimage, one sets self completely aside and opens the heart to all that God has to offer. While it's likely that a pilgrimage will at least period-ically be "fun," that's not the primary goal. The goal is to remove oneself from daily life and its comforts and become submerged in the spiritual dimension. Joyful, yes, because our hearts can't help but be joyful when they rest in God. But it is a deep and profound joy that transforms.

Marian pilgrimages have an added dimension in that they draw us closer to the Mother of our Lord, whom Jesus entrusted to the disciple John as he hung dying on the Cross: "Meanwhile, stand-ing near the cross of Jesus were his mother, and his mother's sister, Mary the wife of Clopas, and Mary Magdalene. When Jesus saw his mother and the disciple whom he loved standing beside her, he said to his mother, 'Woman, here is your son.' Then he said to the disciple, 'Here is your mother.' And from that hour the disciple took her into his own home" (Jn 19:25–27).

As Catholics, we believe that St. John repre-sented all children of God and that Jesus intended for Mary to be truly our Mother and for us to be truly her children. When we make a pilgrimage to a place dedicated to Mary, we honor her and also our Lord since this was his dying request.

Each Marian pilgrimage site shows Mary in a different way and under a different title. She's the same woman, presented uniquely in each place. Yet all Marian pilgrimage sites have one thing in common: from each one, Mary calls her children to herself and distributes graces in abundance to them. From these graces stem spiritual miracles of conversion, healing, comfort, and transformation. In many cases there are physical miracles of cures as well as the solving of many kinds of problems.

Visiting Marian places of grace is ingrained in me. From my earliest years, I've been drawn to our Blessed Mother. That's no credit to me—it's the result of her having called me to herself and showering me with her motherly love and protection. When I was one year old, I was given the great gift of having been consecrated to Mary by Servant of God and founder of the Apostolic Movement of Schoenstatt, Fr. Joseph Kentenich. For those unfamiliar with this custom, consecration to Mary means to place oneself—or someone else—under her special protection and guidance. In a sense, it's asking Mary to claim that person for herself now and for always. Of course, when Mary "claims" someone for herself, she also claims

that person for her Son because the two are insep-
arable. The only reason for Mary's existence is to
lead us to Jesus!

Fr. Kentenich's consecration of me to Mary
was my introduction to the Schoenstatt movement and, especially, to the Schoenstatt Marian
shrine near my childhood home. At the time of the
consecration, Fr. Kentenich presented my mother
with a print of the image of Mary that is enthroned
in every Schoenstatt Marian shrine throughout
the world (260 and counting!), titled the "Mother
Thrice Admirable." Mom hung the picture in our
living room, and I fell in love with it—and with our
Blessed Mother! The connection with the image in
my living room and the image in the Schoenstatt
shrines profoundly impacted me, and the shrine
became home to me. I visited it as often as I could,
spending hours praying, thinking, and sometimes
simply looking into her beautiful eyes. Visiting
Mary in her special place became as natural and
necessary to me as breathing.

As an adult, my love for the Schoenstatt shrine
fostered my love for, and curiosity about, Marian places of grace in general. *Where else is Mary
present? In what ways?* I searched and discovered
that there are innumerable Marian places of grace
throughout the United States. The pilgrimage

places abroad are stunning and viable, but just as stunning and viable are the ones right on American soil. Sadly, far too many remain, for the most part, undiscovered and have receded to the background.

Just before I set out on the final stop of my pilgrimage, I received some tragic news. The Schoenstatt shrine near my childhood home—the one I had come to love so dearly and in which I had spent so many hours in childhood and beyond—was scheduled for demolition. The shrine had been built on parish property and owned by the parish. Located in a declining area, the parish had dwindled, the school enrollment had decreased, and the shrine had fewer and fewer visitors. The hard decision was made to sell the property, and a chain of secular private schools bought it with the intention to raze the buildings and build a new structure to fit their needs. The shrine wasn't important to them; it had to go. The Schoenstatt movement offered a final Mass there at the shrine, with the removal of the Blessed Sacrament as a finale. I cried bitterly, and the tears are still quick to flow whenever I think about it.

Through that tragedy, the Blessed Mother instilled in my heart a fourth dimension of my

Marian pilgrimage: *What happened to the Schoen-statt Marian shrine of my childhood could happen to other Marian places of grace as well.* Secularism is spreading across our country, and no place is completely immune from its clutches. If, by my journeys, I can move others to take interest and ownership in Mary's special places of grace in the United States, perhaps we can turn the tide and save other Marian pilgrimage places from demolition. They are treasures, part of our Catholic heritage in the United States, and that makes them a part of us. It's time to step out of ourselves and into an encounter with our Lord and his Mother—for our own sakes and for the sake of our nation.

In the process of becoming acquainted with the Schoenstatt shrine and movement, I learned a prayer of consecration to Mary and have chosen that as the framework for this novena. It's so simple and childlike that it fits perfectly with the theme of reconquering ourselves and our country for Mary and her Son. The Schoenstatt movement calls it the "Little Consecration." Written by Jesuit Nicolaus Zucchi in the seventeenth century, the Little Consecration has become central to the movement and has been adopted by many people not even associated with Schoenstatt.

My Queen, My Mother,

I give myself entirely to you. And to show my devotion to you, I consecrate to you this day my eyes, my ears, my mouth, my heart, my entire self without reserve. As I am your own, my good Mother, guard me and defend me as your property and possession. Amen.

How to Pray a Living Novena

A novena is a form of Catholic devotion that involves offering special prayers or services for nine consecutive days (*novena* comes from the Latin word for "nine") for a particular intention. This practice can be traced back to apostolic times, when the apostles and Mary gathered in the Upper Room for nine days after the Lord ascended to heaven (see Acts 1–2). On the tenth day, the Holy Spirit descended upon them at Pentecost. Over time, particular novenas dedicated to specific saints or for particular seasons or intentions began to spring up in every time and place.

This book offers a unique kind of prayer experience, a "living novena" or kind of extended guided meditation. By reading one chapter of the book each day, you will experience a kind of "armchair pilgrimage," following my journeys as I traveled across the United States visiting Marian places of grace that are part of our country's history and Catholic heritage.

As we explore one of these holy places each day, the physical landscape of the United States, the historical accounts, and the impressions, experiences, and graces will guide you in discovering signs from the pilgrim's path.

Then, we'll journey deeper into the heart of Mary as we pray for healing of the unfortunate divisions, the hostilities, and even the godlessness that have become so prevalent in our country, as well as the confusion and divisions that have plagued the Church worldwide. We'll offer our petitions and pray for renewed faith, a united and holy Church, and a renewed love of our nation and pride in its Catholic heritage. Finally, we'll consecrate ourselves and our country to the Blessed Virgin Mary, invoking her grace and protection.

At the end of each chapter you'll find questions for meditation. I encourage you to bring these into your prayer time and open yourself to the working of the Holy Spirit in your heart and soul. It can be intimidating to be frank with ourselves and to truthfully admit what's going on inside us. But, unless we do that, we'll never be able to reconquer ourselves and our country for our Blessed Mother and her Son.

I pray that this pilgrimage will be the path through which you better appreciate our country's Catholic roots and places of grace, grow closer to Mary, become stronger in the faith, and receive the answers to your petitions. May this book be your backpack and your rosary be your walking stick on the journey.

In her Immaculate Heart,
Marge Fenelon

DAY ONE

Shrine of Our Lady of La Leche

ST. AUGUSTINE, FLORIDA

It's funny how we can think we know someone well and then one day discover something new that completely changes our perception of that person. After we got engaged, I learned that my husband had spent a summer working at a carnival in a tourist town when he was a young adult. He and his brother had worked one of the cotton candy stands! The thought of my normally reserved and analytical husband swirling clouds of multicolored confection and calling out, "Get your cotton candy here!" sent me into peals of laughter. It was a side of him I never imagined existed. I'm sure he was good at it and enjoyed himself while working, but this unexpected discovery dramatically changed my perception of him.

That can happen with places, too. For example, you can visit the same park dozens of times and never notice the lovely creek with the little footbridge crossing it in the back corner. You wonder how you could have missed it. Yet you did because you thought you knew everything there was to know about that park. We can think we know everything about our amazing country as well. We've studied its history, traveled around, and kept tabs on the national news. What more is there to learn? Then, one day, something pops up that surprises us.

Signs from the Pilgrim's Path

I had a surprise like that when I visited the Shrine of Our Lady of La Leche in St. Augustine, Florida. Since childhood, I've celebrated Thanksgiving with my family each year on the fourth Thursday of November along with the rest of the United States. I knew the story of the first Thanksgiving—how the pilgrims sailed over the ocean on the *Mayflower* seeking religious freedom, how they had suffered, how the Native Americans helped them, and how they gathered for a marvelous feast to celebrate the first harvest. I thought I knew it all, but I didn't.

On September 8, 1565—the same day the city of St. Augustine was founded—Spanish explorer Pedro Menéndez de Avilés landed on the eastern shore of what is now the state of Florida and claimed the site for Spain and the Church. Menéndez was captain general of the Indies Fleet and brought with him colonists and soldiers. He also brought with him a Spanish diocesan priest named Fr. Francisco Lopez de Mendoza Grajales, the fleet's chaplain. Upon landing, Menéndez claimed the land and founded *Mission de Nombre de Dios* (Mission in the Name of God), and Fr. Lopez offered a Mass of thanksgiving at a makeshift altar on the shore. This was the first Catholic Mass ever celebrated on what is now the United States of America.[1]

After the Mass, Pedro Menéndez hosted a wonderful feast for his companions and new native friends, the Timucuans. This became the first permanent Christian settlement in our country.

The thanksgiving feast held by Pedro Menéndez, his companions, the chaplain, and the Timucuans beat the English pilgrims' celebration by fifty-six years! Why haven't we heard of this before? Speculation holds that it's because of the eventual English dominance on this continent and the spread of the English language. The story of the English pilgrims' feast at Plymouth took precedence over the founding of St. Augustine by the Spanish explorers. Regardless, the fact that the first thanksgiving feast in the United States actually took place in Florida decades before the one primarily associated with our national holiday changed my perception of the holiday.

When they came, the Spaniards brought with them a special devotion to the Blessed Virgin Mary. Inspired by the date of their landing—the Nativity of Mary—in 1609 they built a chapel and dedicated it to Our Lady of La Leche (Our Lady of the Milk and Happy Delivery, a title that is believed to have been brought to Spain by the crusaders in the Middle Ages). It dates back to a fourth-century grotto in Bethlehem where Mary is said to have nursed her child. When some of our Lady's milk accidentally spilled, the entire grotto turned white; hence it was named the Milk Grotto. It's believed that is how Mary came to be known as Our Lady of La Leche. During the reign of Philip III of Spain, a miracle was granted through the intercession of Our Lady of La Leche when the lives of a woman and her baby who were expected to die in childbirth were spared. Philip III commissioned a statue to be made of Our Lady of La Leche, and it won the hearts of the Spanish people. The statue shows the Blessed Mother sitting with great love and dignity and tenderly nursing the Infant Jesus. Soon after Menéndez and his men established Mission de Nombre de Dios, Franciscan missionaries from Spain joined them, bringing with them a replica of the statue of Our Lady of La Leche. They built a chapel on the mission grounds and enshrined the statue in it. This became the first Marian shrine in the United States.[2]

The devotion to Our Lady of La Leche spread rapidly among the Timucua, Guale, and Apalache Native Americans who lived in that area, and it continued to spread as more explorers and colonists came to the land. As our country expanded and developed, the area ceased to function as a mission per se, but the grounds and chapel continued to be maintained and other features and structures were added. It became a popular place to go for solitude and prayer. When a hurricane destroyed the chapel in 1923, volunteers rebuilt it in its original form. The shrine has since become the center of devotion for thousands of women who come to pray for our Lady's intercession in difficulties of motherhood, including infertility, raising children, and more. On an almost daily basis, women appear at the shrine to offer thanksgiving for petitions granted regarding pregnancy and childbearing. Additionally, men and women of all walks of life arrive, seeking the consolation and intercession of this most tender of mothers in a vast array of concerns. While none have been formally investigated by the Church, anecdotal evidence says Our Lady of La Leche is performing miracles from her shrine on a regular basis.[3]

The first thing I learned when I reached the shrine was that Mass would begin in a little while. That I could attend Mass at the site of the first ever celebrated in my home country was a tremendous and unexpected blessing! My heart was so full of gratitude that I could barely think of anything else. Although I know this not to be the case, it felt as though that Mass was held just for me. It happened to be the Feast of St. Mark, my husband's patron saint, and this was an added blessing. In the homily, the priest spoke of St. Mark's mission and subsequent suffering and pointed out that we all have a mission and all are called to suffering in imitation of our Lord. Then he said something that will stay with me always. Regarding suffering, he said, "The real question is, 'Who are you becoming in the midst of your suffering?'" I had never thought of it that way before. Surely there was suffering for the Menéndez company as they forged their way in this unknown territory. Look who they became in their suffering!

Walking the grounds of the shrine, I found it easy to imagine what it was like in 1565 when Menéndez, Fr. Lopez, and their companions first set foot there. Their landing spot is marked by the Great Cross, a 208-foot stainless steel cross representing the no-longer-standing large cross erected by Fr. Lopez upon his arrival. Across a small creek is a life-size bronze statue of the Spanish priest, his arms extended in praise of God. A few yards away is a replica of the makeshift altar upon which the first Mass was offered. Standing at the shore near the cross, I caught myself taking long, deep breaths—not because I needed extra oxygen but rather because I wanted to breathe in the ocean air just as Pedro Menéndez and Fr. Lopez had done. I wanted to breathe in God's glory and the fervency of their mission to spread Christianity to all shores. I stood straight and spread my arms in imitation of the bronze image of Fr. Lopez. I heard the voices of the soldiers, colonists, and Timucuans—the prayers of praise and thanksgiving, the laughter, the chatter. I heard the clatter of the dishes and the crackling of the cooking fires. For that moment, I

felt the joy of the real first thanksgiving celebration
in the United States.

From there, I strolled along the pathways that
wind throughout the beautifully landscaped property. I stopped before the statues of the many saints
who are honored there, walked the Stations of the
Cross, and paused at the spot of the first Mass on
US soil. I wondered what my life might be like if
the Catholic faith had never been brought here by
the courageous men and women who sacrificed
so much for the glory of God. I looked around me,
seeing in my mind's eye the weary soldiers, hel-
mets under their arms, hands folded, and kneeling
to receive our Lord in the Eucharist. I pictured the
priest's sacred hands gently placing the Host on
each tongue, and I imagined Menéndez kneeling
to the side, head bowed in deep gratitude. I, too,
bowed my head in gratitude.

Not far from the altar, two archeological exca-
vations are being conducted by the University of
Florida. Since the project began in 1993, the archeological team has unearthed some of the most
important discoveries in the history of St. Augustine, including a moat believed to belong to the
structure that Menéndez built. What else have they
discovered? What else will they discover as they
proceed with excavation? Perhaps there might be

vessels used for holy Mass or shards of equipment handled by the Spanish soldiers. Maybe deep in the earth are remnants of the Great Cross Fr. Lopez built and raised.

I saved my visit to the chapel of Our Lady of La Leche for last. Admittedly, that was doing things somewhat backward since it's the shrine's main attraction, so to speak, but I didn't want my time there interrupted by a rush to see the other features on the grounds before they closed for the day. I wanted to have the opportunity to sit quietly, take it all in, and pour my heart out to my Mother.

That's exactly what I did.

The chapel is small and simple, yet it is exquisite. It's simply furnished, with a votive candle stand in the back, Stations of the Cross on the side walls, wooden benches, and a plain wooden altar in the front. Humble stained-glass windows let in a splash of sunlight. The chapel's simplicity adds to its allure while at the same time compelling those who enter to focus on the beautiful statue of Our Lady of La Leche, which rests on a pedestal in an alcove behind the altar. Once I'd entered, I couldn't take my eyes off her. I'm almost embarrassed to admit that I initially balked at the thought of a statue of Mary nursing—it seemed so foreign to me. I've seen images and imagined Mary doing many different things as a wife and mother, and I know that she lived an ordinary life just as we do. It makes perfect sense that she would have nursed our Lord because it's a natural thing for mothers to do for their infants. Still, I never considered something so private and intimate between Mother and Child. But Our Lady of La Leche is so graceful and modest, so tender and loving that it seems perfectly natural. I couldn't resist gazing at her peaceful and reassuring face.

I sat there in silence for a little more than an hour, and in that time, several young women came in, knelt to pray, and left after a short while. A handful of them were in tears. I had no idea what they'd come in to pray for, but I was immediately drawn to pray for whatever it was and to entrust them to our Lady. Strangely, it felt as though I was supposed to be there right at that time and was expected to pray for them. In this moment, that was my calling.

Viewing Our Interior Landscape

Have you ever discovered something completely new about a person or place you knew well that surprised you? Depending on what you discovered, it most likely would have either delighted or confused you. Perhaps both. It even could have irritated you. We don't usually like to have our preconceived notions challenged, preferring instead to remain in a state of self-satisfied certainty. This is especially true of our prejudices and biases. Whether we realize it or not, we all have them and for the most part, we're reticent to let go of them out of fear or pride. If you're completely honest with yourself, you'll see that you hang onto thinking patterns that aren't entirely based on truth. That's part of human weakness. It's easy to get stuck in the rut of your perceptions and to think that you know all there is to know. If you can bring yourself to be open-minded, you'll be able to look again with fresh eyes. Prayer and frequent reception of the sacraments are safeguards against notions that can become sinful.

It seems lots of people think they know all there is to know about the United States, especially if they've lived here over a prolonged period. Because of that, they act out of a mindset that may not be accurately informed and can get stuck in a perception of our country that is negative and based on skepticism. Skepticism leads to ingratitude, ingratitude leads to ridicule, and ridicule leads to hopelessness. Once hopelessness sets in, we don't even bother to look for anything to appreciate about our homeland. Do you have a tendency toward that kind of thinking?

We would all do well to meditate on the attitude of the Menéndez company as they claimed this land for the Church, offered the first Catholic Mass on US soil, and gathered with the Timucuans for a thanksgiving feast! They had great hope for this land, a hope that they prayed would not diminish over the centuries to come. We need to pray for that same hope.

The Journey Begins

Offer yourself, your loved ones, and our country to Mary, asking her intercession that an attitude of genuine thanksgiving may fill your heart and the hearts of all the people of the United States. Then consecrate yourself and our nation to the Blessed Virgin Mary.

My Queen, My Mother,

I give myself entirely to you. And to show my devotion to you, I consecrate to you this day, my eyes, my ears, my mouth, my heart, my entire self without reserve. As I am your own, my good Mother, guard me and defend me as your property and possession. Amen.

Pray the Rosary for those who have fallen into negativism and skepticism. Pray also for the leaders of our country that they may guide us with wisdom and godly principles.

Stepping Out in Faith

- Have you ever discovered something about someone you love that changed how you saw them? How did you handle it?

- Have you caught yourself in a snarl of skepticism and ridicule about our country? What brought you out of it? If you're still caught, what can you do to pull yourself out of it?

- How do you respond to others who become skeptical and negative? What can you say or do to help them reach toward real thanksgiving?

DAY TWO

National Shrine of Our Lady of Prompt Succor

NEW ORLEANS, LOUISIANA

Americans love independence. We fought to gain it in the Revolutionary War (1775–1783) as we battled to break from British rule. We wanted to be able to stand on our own two feet, so to speak, and to ensure that our freedoms would not be infringed upon by another. Many colonists came to this country to secure their ability to practice their faith without persecution or constriction, and they weren't about to let that be taken away. As a nation, we again fought to maintain our independence in the War of 1812 when we became

caught in the conflict between England and France
as Napoleon Bonaparte waged his campaign for
world dominance. Because of that, the War of 1812
is often referred to as the "second war of independence." It's our American indomitability that has
kept us independent to this day.

Signs from the Pilgrim's Path

Surprisingly, the most remarkable battle of the
War of 1812 happened *after* the war had ended. On
December 24, 1814, Great Britain and the United
States signed a treaty that essentially ended the
war. These were the days long before cell phones
and internet, and news traveled slowly. It took a
long time for word to get across the ocean that
the conflict had ended. Without knowledge of the
treaty, the British and American soldiers believed
they were still at war. On January 8, 1815, the two
sides met in what turned out to be the War of
1812's most decisive engagements—the bloody
Battle of New Orleans. Future American president Andrew Jackson led a misfit band of mili-
tia fighters, frontiersmen, farmers, slaves, Native
Americans, and even pirates in an attack against
the superior British forces. They were vastly out-
numbered and severely underequipped, yet they
managed to inflict devastating casualties on their

opponents, and they won the battle against all odds. The Battle of New Orleans foiled the plans for British invasion of the American frontier and boosted Jackson to lasting national fame.[1]

History books don't record one of the most important background details of the battle, however. As the British army of nearly 10,000 soldiers was advancing toward New Orleans, the Americans, with only cotton bales for fortifications, awaited them. The women of the city fled to the Ursuline Convent chapel and spent the night there with the nuns, praying before the statue of Our Lady of Prompt Succor. There was a rumor that General Jackson would set the city ablaze rather than let the British capture it. On the morning of January 8, the vicar-general celebrated Mass on the main altar. Before the Mass ended, a messenger appeared to announce that the battle was over and had been won by Jackson and his troops. The battle in its entirety had lasted less than twenty minutes! Jackson, who was not a believer, went to the convent to personally thank the Ursulines for their prayers, sharing a special supper with them in celebration and thanksgiving. He admitted that there most certainly was a "divine interposition" in the battle.[2]

In a January 19, 1815, letter addressed to Louisiana bishop Guillaume DuBourg and intended for the Ursuline sisters, Jackson wrote, "The signal interposition of Heaven in giving success to our arms against the enemy, who so lately landed on our shores—while it must excite in every bosom attached to the happy government under which we live emotions of the liveliest gratitude, requires at the same time some external manifestation of those feelings."

Extraordinary! Even a skeptic had to admit that prayer can and does affect the course of history. It's through the prayers of the Ursulines and the intercession of Our Lady of Prompt Succor that the Battle of New Orleans was miraculously won and our American independence was preserved for future generations—the same independence that we enjoy today.

According to Ursuline annals, this was the second time that Our Lady of Prompt Succor had interceded for New Orleans. In 1788, a great fire ravaged the city, and the wind drove the flames directly toward the Ursuline Convent and adjacent buildings. Before leaving the convent, one of the sisters placed a small statue of our Lady on a windowsill facing the fire. At the same time, another sister prayed aloud, "Our dear Lady, come quickly to our help or we are lost." At that moment, the wind changed direction and the Ursuline property and the rest of New Orleans was spared. The Ursulines still own this statue, which became known as "Sweetheart" and has a place of honor in a small side chapel of the shrine. Anecdotal evidence says that countless miracles have taken place through her intercession, particularly a long list of soldiers whom Sweetheart brought home safely from war.[3]

Andrew Jackson isn't the only president of the United States who held a special place in his heart for the Ursulines. When the Louisiana Purchase was negotiated, the Ursulines became concerned. That tract of land had formally belonged to France—a country and government with which they were familiar. They were not at all familiar with the United States and its government, and so when the territory became US property, they worried what might happen to them. Would they be persecuted for their Catholic faith? Would they be forced to surrender their property and abandon the school? What would happen to the students? These were all questions that needed answers, and so the Mother Superior wrote to then-president of the United States, Thomas Jefferson, inquiring about his intentions for them and pleading their case. On May 15, 1804, they received a response from the president himself.

He wrote, "I have received, good sisters, the letter you have written me wherein you express anxiety for the property vested in your institution by the former governments of Louisiana. The principles of the Constitution and government of the United States are a sure guarantee to you that it will be preserved to you sacred and inviolate, and that your institution will be permitted to govern itself according to its own voluntary rules, without interference from the civil authority."

He ended the letter by offering appreciation and gratitude for the work of the Ursulines and assuring them that "it will meet all the protection which my office can give it. I salute you, holy sisters, with friendship and respect."[4]

The story of how the Ursulines established their order in New Orleans is miraculous itself and is also attributed to the intercession of Our Lady of Prompt Succor. The French Ursulines came to New Orleans in 1727 and founded a school for girls. (It's the oldest currently operating girls' school in the United States.) In 1803, a crisis caused a group of the nuns to flee to Cuba. One of the remaining nuns, Mother St. Andre Madier, appealed to her cousin in France, Mother St. Michel Gensoul—also an Ursuline—for help.

Mother St. Michel was a remarkable woman with great talent, interior piety, and firm resolve. Upon receiving her cousin's request for help, Mother St. Michel petitioned Bishop Fournier of Montpelier, France, for permission to travel to New Orleans, but he refused. To make things harder, he told Mother St. Michel that only the pope could grant such a request. However, the pope at that time was a prisoner of the emperor Napoleon!

Still, that did not subdue the brave nun's resolve; she petitioned the pope in a letter. Then one day, while praying before a statue of the Blessed Virgin Mary, Mother St. Michel received divine inspiration: "O most holy Virgin Mary, if you obtain a prompt and favorable answer to my letter, I promise to have you honored in New Orleans under the title of Our Lady of Prompt Succor."[5]

This promise must have pleased Mary very much, because she in turn granted special favors. One notable favor was that the pope replied quickly to Mother St. Michel's letter, praising her generosity and faith and approving her departure for New Orleans. In gratitude, Mother St. Michel commissioned a statue under the title Our Lady of Prompt Succor, and the surprised Bishop Fournier asked to bless it once it was completed. Devotion to *Notre Dame de Prompt Secourse* spread quickly, and in 1810, the statue Mother St. Michel had brought from France was enthroned in the Ursuline Convent chapel in the French Quarter of New Orleans. Bishop Fournier loved Our Lady of Prompt Succor and the Ursuline sisters so much that he willed that, upon his death, his heart be entombed in the Ursuline mausoleum at the shrine.[6]

In 1895, the statue—now gilded in gold—was crowned by Decree of His Holiness Pope Leo XIII, and in 1928, the Holy See approved and confirmed the naming of Our Lady of Prompt Succor as the principal patronness of the city of New Orleans and the state of Louisiana.[7]

Through the centuries, Our Lady of Prompt Succor has continued her work, bringing quick help to those who seek her aid. Visitors from all over the world have come to the shrine, and it's common to see the faithful kneeling or resting in the pews as they pour out their hearts to her. Given this, it's no surprise to hear sniffling and quiet sobs of those in distress. Like the courageous woman who brought her there, Our Lady of Prompt Succor is a woman of resolve who came for a purpose and remains to carry it out—granting quick help to all who turn to her.

Sitting in the shrine on a warm spring afternoon, I mulled over all that I had learned that morning. I couldn't decide what impressed me the most. Was it the courage of the Ursulines? Was it the miraculous intercession of Our Lady of Prompt Succor? Was it an obscure little statue of Mary called Sweetheart and the protection she has offered to so many? It all impressed me, and as I reviewed each story in my head, they impressed me even more. Still, I kept coming back to the story of Andrew Jackson and the miracle of the Battle of New Orleans. Our Lady of Prompt Succor had directly intervened in preserving the freedom of our country and assuring our continued independence. That wasn't a coincidence, some random action because Mary felt like being nice that day. No, she interceded with purpose. She interceded because she's interested in the events of US history and she cares about its people.

As I prayed there, I had an epiphany. I've often wondered why Mary has so many titles in so many different shrines and has appeared in so many ways. Why isn't she the same everywhere? The answer came to me: She *is* the same everywhere but she also has an array of amazing aspects. Our Lord Jesus desired that we honor her and appreciate all her different gifts and attributes. She doesn't divide or change herself, and she doesn't want to confuse us. She comes to us under her different titles to show the many sides of herself and to touch the heart of every one of her children, who are as varied and unique as are her qualities and powers.

Just as a mother shows different sides of herself to her children depending on the personality and needs of the child, so Mary does for us. A mother might be playful with her younger children and more serious with her older ones. She might be firm with the naughty ones but gentle with the hurting ones. She's careful with the timid ones and assuring with the doubtful ones, nurturing with the tiny ones and perhaps rough-and-tumble with the raucous ones. Our divine Mother comes to us in the way and at the time that we need her most. I had never understood it so clearly until that moment sitting in the shrine of Our Lady of Prompt Succor!

Viewing Our Interior Landscape

Think about the last time your travel plans were usurped by inclement weather. Most likely, you were irritated, at least for a while. Maybe you planned on doing something important but were blocked by someone in authority over you. Did you like it? Probably not. Or perhaps there's a rule that you don't agree with for whatever reason. You might obey it, but begrudgingly. If you are like most Americans, you value your independence. None of us want that taken away.

Our independence is importance to us for reasons beyond the satisfaction of our rebelliousness. We must be left free to follow God's will for us as individuals and as a Church in keeping with our Catholic beliefs. Genuine independence means having the ability to discern what God wants us to do and how he wishes us to act despite our environment and pressures to conduct ourselves differently. Have you ever felt pressure to be someone other than who you really are? Our Lady of Prompt Succor can help. Not only will she assist you in material and physical needs but she also will give you quick help in spiritual needs as well. Reaching out to her when you come under pressure to surrender your independence can effect real change in your life. Like the Ursuline sisters when the fire of New Orleans loomed, you can pray, "Our dear Lady, come quickly to my help, or I am lost." She will hear and answer your prayer.

What about our country? We can choose when and where to go and for how long. We can worship

God, participate in holy Mass, and cling to our system of beliefs. We're not under the dominion of a foreign government but rather have our own governance. Day after day, we can conduct our lives in peace and freedom. Yet when events prevent us from exercising our wills exactly as we wish we can often forget how much freedom and independence we really have here in the United States. Do you sometimes forget about that?

The Journey Begins

Offer yourself, your loved ones, and our country to Mary, asking her intercession that an attitude of godly indomitability may fill your heart and the hearts of all the people of the United States. Then consecrate yourself and our nation to the Blessed Virgin Mary.

My Queen, My Mother,

I give myself entirely to you. And to show my devotion to you, I consecrate to you this day, my eyes, my ears, my mouth, my heart, my entire self without reserve. As I am your own, my good Mother, guard me and defend me as your property and possession. Amen.

Pray the Rosary for those who no longer have confidence in our nation's indomitability. Pray also for the leaders of our country that they may guide us with wisdom and godly principles.

Stepping Out in Faith

- What does independence mean to you? What does it look like for you on a day-to-day basis?

- Why do you think Mary takes an interest in our American history?

- What can you do to help yourself and others to be more appreciative of the freedom and independence we have in the United States?

- Under which title or titles is Mary speaking to you now? Why?

DAY THREE

St. Mary's Mission and Museum

STEVENSVILLE, MONTANA

The United States has a legacy of freedom, but it also has a legacy of expansion. Generation by generation, we reached across the continent—to the Appalachian Mountains after the Revolutionary War, into the South and across the prairie lands of the Midwest, on to the Rocky Mountains, and finally, to the Pacific Coast. Americans believed that it was God's will, their "Manifest Destiny," that the United States control the North American continent from Atlantic to Pacific.[1] From a Catholic

perspective, this "destiny" also meant Christianizing the continent.

Signs from the Pilgrim's Path

Part of Christianizing the continent meant bringing
the Catholic faith to Native Americans. As we'll
read about on day seven, the Europeans and their
new religion weren't always welcome, and many
missionaries were martyred. The Native Americans were suspicious of first the Europeans and
later the Americans and their God. It didn't help,
either, that Native American homelands and traditions were threatened by American expansion.
However, not all tribes were opposed to the foreign visitors. In fact, many welcomed the settlers,
offering them assistance and friendship and even
eventually embracing the Catholic faith through
the teachings of the missionaries.

In the Bitterroot Valley of the Rocky Mountains, it was not the missionaries' teachings that
brought the Catholic faith to the local Native
Americans but rather Native Americans from
other tribes.

In the early 1800s, twenty-four members of an
Iroquois tribe arrived in the northwestern United
States as part of the Hudson's Bay Company. In the
Rocky Mountain valley along the Bitterroot River,

they met the Salish tribe, known as the Flatheads among people of European descent, and quickly became friends with them. During the 1823–1824 trapping season, twelve of the Iroquois remained among the Salish in the Bitterroot Valley. The Iroquois were adopted into the Salish tribe and married members of the tribe. These Iroquois came from a people who had converted to Christianity more than 200 years earlier; they were eager to share their faith with their new Salish friends.[2]

The Salish and their neighbors, the Nez Percé, became intrigued with what the Iroquois told them about the Catholic faith and priests. They were so interested in the priests and their teachings that they wanted them to come to live among the tribe to instruct them in Christianity. In 1831, they sent three of their chiefs to St. Louis, Missouri, to find priests and ask them to return with them to the village. Sadly, all three chiefs died of sickness. When they didn't return to the tribe for extended time, five others were appointed to journey to St. Louis after them. Tragically, all five were massacred as they tried to pass through the territory of the Sioux. In 1834, a third delegation set out, this time accompanied by an Iroquois brave and his two children. This delegation was successful in making the 3,000-mile trek to St. Louis, only to discover that there were not enough missionaries to return with them. Resolute in their purpose, the Salish sent a final delegation to St. Louis in 1839. This delegation was successful.[3]

In St. Louis, the delegation met Fr. Pierre-Jean De Smet, a Jesuit missionary who longed to take the Catholic faith to the frontier. He assured the Salish that he would come and requested permission from his order's superiors and the bishop. Permission was granted, and Fr. De Smet set out immediately for the Salish village to assess the possibility of founding a mission there. Upon reaching the village, Fr. De Smet discovered a people yearning for Christianity.

Before winter set in, Fr. De Smet traveled to Fort Colville of the Hudson's Bay Company to obtain supplies for the winter plus wheat, oats, potatoes, and garden seeds for the first crops. He also brought with him Montana's first cattle, swine, and poultry. He remained with the Salish for about three months, instructing them in the catechism, teaching them prayers, and baptizing them before returning to St. Louis in December 1840.

He returned the following spring, this time with his fellow Jesuit missionaries—Fr. Gregory Mengarini and Fr. Nicolas Point—plus three Jesuit lay brothers. Their first task was to find a suitable tract of land on which to establish the mission, and they wandered the barren mountains for many days looking for one without success. By God's grace, they found the perfect location for the mission on the Feast of the Nativity of the Blessed Virgin Mary and named the mission St. Mary's in her honor, as well as the river and tallest mountain peak to the west of the mission. In a solemn procession, they erected a cross on the land. Soon after, they built a chapel and other buildings to accommodate their needs. This became the first white settlement in what would later become the state of Montana and, because of this, St. Mary's Mission is touted as "the place where Montana began."[4]

News spread of the priests' arrival, and before long, Native Americans from other tribes came to visit the mission, necessitating the building of a larger chapel. In all, four chapels would be built there—each one replacing its predecessor either because of the growing numbers of converted Native Americans or destruction due to flooding or fires. The chapel on the property today dates to 1923 but contains furnishings and statuary dating to the mission's early years.

The greatest developments of St. Mary's Mission came at the hands of Fr. Anthony Ravalli, an Italian Jesuit sent to serve at the mission in 1845. Highly educated, he was an accomplished artist, architect, sculptor, engineer, woodworker, surgeon, pharmacist, musician, and agriculturalist.[5] Fr. Ravalli quickly won the hearts of the Salish, teaching them the faith but also skills, including agricultural and farming methods. He even formed a musical band among the Salish that played scores by German and Italian composers![6]

In 1850, in response to escalating hostility from the Blackfoot tribe—enemies of the Salish—the mission was evacuated and transferred farther down the river to Fort Owen.[7] St. Mary's remained vacant until 1866 when the Jesuits sent Fr. Ravalli back to reestablish the mission.[8] The property was further developed with the addition of a study, dining room, and kitchen, and a one-and-a-half-story barn adjacent to the chapel, which was doubled in size in 1879 to fit the growing needs of the community. Fr. Ravalli built the furnishings for the buildings himself using materials that were salvaged, recycled, and, in rare cases, purchased or traded from Fort Owen's trading post.[9]

As westward expansion spread and both settlers and government agencies moved into the area, the US government took possession of Native American lands and signed a treaty with the Salish requiring them to move to the Jocko Reservation, where tracts of land would be assigned to them and they would be granted materials, equipment, and livestock for farming. The Jesuits stayed, continuing to serve the Salish, but it was clear that St. Mary's Mission as it was once known was winding down. In 1891, the Salish chief reluctantly signed a final agreement for the last of the Salish to relocate to the reservation under the condition that his people be cared for adequately there, would be able to return on pilgrimage annually, and that the Salish burial grounds (now St. Mary's Cemetery) be kept sacred.[10] His conditions were granted, although the Salish continued to suffer poverty on the reservation. After that, St. Mary's became a mission for white settlers and subsequently became St. Mary's parish in 1921.[11] In 1954, a new parish church was built, and St. Mary's Mission became a museum with all of the original furnishings and decorations authentically restored and kept exactly as they had been when Fr. Ravalli was there. Yet it's more than a museum; it's a monument to the Salish who sought Christianity and the brave Jesuits who brought it to them.

Two apparitions are said to have taken place at St. Mary's. Neither have been approved by the Church, and both occurred sometime after Fr. De Smet's return to the mission in 1841. The first involved a man named Michael, a member of the Cree tribe, who saw St. Francis Xavier appear to him while at prayer in the chapel.[12] The second was documented by Fr. De Smet. A twelve-year-old Salish boy named Paul saw the Blessed Virgin Mary in a vision. He had been struggling to learn his catechism lessons and seemed incapable of committing them to memory in time for the Christmas celebrations. Distraught, Paul went to the lodge of one of the catechists to seek help. Upon entering, he saw a beautiful woman hovering about two feet above the ground and surrounded by a bright light. She was dressed in white with a sphere, half moon, and a serpent with a "strange fruit in its mouth" beneath her feet. There was a bright star above her head, and her heart was somehow visible with streams of light coming forth from it. At first, Paul was afraid, but the woman's smile calmed his fears. He asked the woman to teach him his prayers, and suddenly his mind cleared and he was able to recite all of his catechisms without trouble. He could repeat his catechisms to perfection from then on.[13]

Fr. Ravalli created a painting of Paul's apparition that hangs on the wall inside of St. Mary's Chapel today. Of all the fascinating features of St. Mary's Mission, the story of Paul and the painting by Fr. Ravalli most capture my heart. It's a beautiful painting, and it proves that Fr. Ravalli was an accomplished artist. The best part of the painting is Paul's face. He gazes up at the Blessed Mother in perfect trust and innocence, completely unpretentious and focused entirely on her. She, in turn, gazes back in limitless love, her eyes filled with assurance and grace. The two seem to belong together. Paul is representative of the entire Salish people. In his humble love and simplicity, he accepted Mary as his Blessed Mother and recognized the good, the true, and the beautiful—that which he yearned for with all his heart.

Viewing Our Interior Landscape

The concept of expansion applies to more than geography and land features; it applies to our souls as well. The Salish sensed that there was something very important about the religion that the Iroquois practiced, and they yearned to learn more about it. They yearned for the expansion of their souls and knew that the Catholic faith was the path for that expansion.

The yearning for spiritual expansion is inherent to all human beings. Regardless of our cultural or religious backgrounds, our souls hunger for the good, true, and beautiful. Long before organized religion, ancient civilizations believed in some sort of god or gods that governed the earth and offered it praise and honor. Intuitively, we know that our souls will expand when we draw closer to the divine.

What about you? Do you sense your yearning to draw closer to God? Do you yearn for the expansion of your soul in the Catholic faith? The Salish sent not one but four search parties to bring back someone who could teach them Catholicism. You do not need to go to such lengths. You can be your own search party, seeking out ways to deepen your knowledge of the Catholic faith and allowing your soul to expand in the gifts and graces the Church has to offer you.

The Journey Begins

Offer yourself, your loved ones, and our country to Mary, asking her intercession that all that is good, true, and beautiful may fill your heart and the hearts of all the people of the United States. Then consecrate yourself and our nation to the Blessed Virgin Mary.

> My Queen, My Mother,
>
> I give myself entirely to you. And to show my devotion to you, I consecrate to you this day, my eyes, my ears, my mouth, my heart, my entire self without reserve. As I am your own, my good Mother, guard me and defend me as your property and possession. Amen.

Pray the Rosary for those who no longer yearn for what is good, true, and beautiful. Pray also for the leaders of our country that they may guide our nation with wisdom and godly principles.

Stepping Out in Faith

- How can you, like little Paul, turn to Mary when struggling to embrace or understand a part of your faith?

- How will you begin your own journey of expansion into the Catholic faith?

- How can you show appreciation for those who have gone before you in a practical and meaningful way?

Shrine of Our Lady of Sorrows

STARKENBURG, MISSOURI

America has often been called a "melting pot" because of the vast array of nationalities and customs that make up our society. Some think that "salad bowl" would be a better metaphor since the cultures of immigrants don't blend or disappear but rather mix together within American culture. Just as in a salad the vegetables keep their flavor and integrity yet form a cohesive dish, so, too, the various cultures retain their integrity and flavor, so to speak, and make one cohesive country. Throughout America's entire history, peoples

41

from foreign shores have come to this land hoping
for a better life than they had in their homelands.
Political unrest in other countries caused a dra-
matic upswing of US immigration in the 1800s.
The majority of immigrants were from Germany
and Ireland, but there also were thousands from
other European countries and also China.[1] When
they came, they brought with them the richness
of their heritage. That richness has added to the
cultural wealth of America.

Signs from the Pilgrim's Path

What follows is the background of the Shrine of
Our Lady of Sorrows in Starkenburg, Missouri. In
1847, immigrant German settlers came from the
neighboring town of Hermann, on the banks of
the Missouri river. The Germans loved this area
because it reminded them of home. There were
no parishes or churches in this newly settled
region, and priests were spread thinly over the
prairielands. They traveled great distances from
community to community to administer the sacraments. When they came to the Starkenburg area,
they'd celebrate Mass and other special services
in a barn that served as a makeshift church. In
the barn, there was a statue of the Blessed Virgin
Mary that the Germans had named the "White

Lady." The statue's origin is unclear. A year after the settlers' arrival, they were granted a charter by the bishop. With the charter, the German immigrants also obtained a forty-acre plot of land. They formed a parish and named it St. Martin's Catholic Church after St. Martin, bishop of Tours, France.[2]

In 1852, the parishioners of St. Martin's built a small log chapel—a new home for the White Lady. As was their custom, the Germans often conducted processions around their extensive property while carrying the White Lady. These processions attracted the attention of the wider community, and soon even non-Catholics would join them.

Twenty years later, the parishioners of St. Martin's decided that the log church was no longer suitable and prepared to build a new one of stone. The cornerstone was laid, and rock was quarried from nearby for the rest of the church. In 1873, Fr. Joseph Schaefer, St. Martin's pastor, placed the White Lady in the newly built Gothic-style church. A year later, it was consecrated.

The parishioners worked hard to import a large bell for the bell tower as well as several statues and stained-glass windows from their homeland. The White Lady remained in the church for a few years but then was replaced with a larger and more elegant one while the original was placed into storage in an attic. In 1887, Fr. George Hoehn became pastor of St. Martin's Church, traveling from his home in Heppenheim, Germany, to assume the position. He was accompanied by his nephew, August Mitsch, who came to serve as the parish sacristan. Fr. Hoehn was enthusiastic and amiable and was impressed by the deep, humble piety of his parishioners.[3]

One day in May, Fr. Hoehn's nephew noticed a lovely dogwood bush in full bloom and was inspired to place beneath the bush an old white statue of Mary that he had found in the corner of an attic. It was the original statue of the White Lady. He set candles around the statue and created a beautiful May altar in honor of the Blessed Virgin Mary. Devotion before this altar became so popular among the parishioners that August and two helpers built a log hut to shelter the White Lady. The hut was so small that only two people could kneel inside and the rest had to kneel on the ground outside.

With an increasing number of faithful visiting the hut, more space was needed, and so the men built a small chapel, also made of logs. It was octagonal-shaped and had a small steeple in front. Stained glass windows and a bell imported from Germany were added. With the approval of the bishop, a Way of the Cross was erected in the adjacent woods on the Feast of the Seven Dolors in 1889. The following year, during Lent, a large donation enabled the parish to purchase a statue of the Sorrowful Mother—a replica of the highly renowned *Pietà of Achtermann* displayed in the Cathedral of Muenster. The Sorrowful Mother statue replaced the White Lady and attracted multitudes of visitors each year.[4]

In 1891, an expansion was added to St. Martin's Church and a dedication ceremony was planned but stalled because of torrential rains that occurred nonstop for nearly six weeks. The rains not only prohibited the dedication but also kept the farmers from harvesting their wheat, threatening their livelihood. Fr. Hoehn remembered a miracle that had once taken place in Germany in which Mary interceded by sending rain to stop a severe drought. Perhaps she could perform the opposite miracle in Starkenburg! That afternoon, the parishioners held a procession and prayed that Mary would stop the rain. The next morning, as well as many following mornings, dawned bright and clear, and the farmers were able to work in their fields.[5]

In 1894, the farmers' fields were again threatened—this time by a severe drought. Crop failure

seemed unavoidable, but the parishioners refused
to admit defeat. They again petitioned their Sorrowful Mother. During the night of June 24, the
log chapel caught fire and all the altar linens and
decorations were destroyed. But the statue and
its white veil—held in place by a wreath made of
wax—remained untouched and the fire ceased
burning. Soon after, the rains fell and the crops
were saved. News of the two miracles traveled
fast, and before long, a steady stream of pilgrims
arrived from areas throughout the Missouri river
and St. Louis regions. The influx of pilgrims neces-
sitated the building of a still larger chapel, which
was begun in 1902. In 1910, the statue of the Sorrowful Mother was enthroned in a side altar of the
new chapel. The original White Lady, now painted
in lovely colors, was enthroned in the chapel as
well, and on September 15—the Feast of Our Lady
of Sorrows—the new chapel was dedicated during
a High Mass followed by a procession through the
woods.[6]

Pilgrims continue to come and miracles continue to happen in Starkenburg through the intercession of the Sorrowful Mother. At the shrine's
side altar are pairs of old wooden crutches
left behind by those who hobbled in and then
walked out after begging our Sorrowful Mother's

intercession. A shoe brace rests there, left behind by a young woman in 1935; she had been infected with polio, and one leg consequently was left shorter than the other. Near the Lourdes grotto at the shrine is a well into which waters from the spring in Lourdes, France, had been added periodically. The woman's parents brought her to the grotto repeatedly over the course of weeks and years, washing her leg in the holy water and praying for a miraculous cure. Finally, with no apparent alternative, the woman was scheduled for surgery to remedy the problem. She was prepped for the procedure, and the surgeon entered the operating room. Surprised, he stopped just as he was about to begin the procedure. There was no need for the surgery, he told his staff. There was absolutely nothing wrong with the young woman's leg! The malady had been cured. In gratitude she brought her shoe brace to our Lady and left it there at her feet in the shrine.

There are many such miracles, and the walls and pillars are covered with engraved stone plaques offering gratitude for favors received. Most of them are inscribed in German and a few in other European languages, with dates that range from the mid-1800s to the end of the 1900s.[7]

As I walked the grounds of the Shrine of Our Lady of Sorrows in Starkenburg, Missouri, it was as if I could hear the whisper of history. Perhaps it was because it was a warm and sunny mid-October day. Perhaps it was because it was a quiet Monday and fewer folks were visiting than during the rest of the week. Perhaps it was the solitude of its rural location. Or perhaps history really *was* whispering to me.

St. Martin's Catholic Church continued to be an active parish until 1979, when it was merged with St. Joseph's Catholic Church in Rhineland to form the Church of the Risen Savior in Rhineland, which continues to administer the site. St. Martin's Catholic Church is no longer used as a worship space and has been converted into a museum with all of the altar linens, decorations, furnishings, and so on kept intact and in place, including the missals and songbooks. It feels as if Sunday Mass might begin at any moment, and it's at once eerie and breathtaking. There is a melancholy spirit there, a memory of old-world traditions and the people who worked so hard to bring the parish to life. The sacristy also is a museum space, with photographs, vestments, Mass vessels, old German hymnals, sacramentals, and artifacts dating all the way back to the original German immigrants. I've seen dozens upon dozens of museums in my travels—many of them religiously themed—but I have never seen one like St. Martin's Catholic Church.

Initially, I found it unsettling. *Why can't this gorgeous church be used for liturgies at least on occasion?* I asked the shrine's historian. She answered, "You wouldn't want to sell such a beautiful church, especially when it once was home to our Lord Jesus Christ in the tabernacle. If you emptied it, where would you go with all of the beautiful furnishings and artifacts? It's such an important part of our heritage here that we didn't want to let go of it. And so we decided to make it into a museum that people could visit so that they could see exactly what a midwest Catholic Church was like in the 1800s."[8]

Then I got it. Turning St. Martin Catholic Church into museum wasn't an act of stowing away the past but of making it accessible to the future. The entire complex is a testimony to the grit, hard work, and devotion of the German immigrants to the area and a tribute to their enduring faith. The grounds of the shrine are stunningly beautiful and enchantingly peaceful. There were other cars in the parking lot the day I visited, but I was never aware of another human presence because everything was enveloped in a sacred

silence. Yet that silence is filled with the voices of
the past, of hearts pouring out their worries, fears,
distress, and gratitude to their Sorrowful Mother.
Our Sorrowful Mother. Walking the grounds, I
merely had to close my eyes to see the German
immigrants—weathered, hopeful, and completely
devoted to our Sorrowful Mother—making their
way in procession over the property. I could hear
the bells ring, summoning the faithful to Mass, and
I could smell the incense from the altar boy's cen-
sor. History came alive for me that day as I nestled
myself into Mary's heart at the Shrine of Our Lady
of Sorrows, and I felt a tangible connection to the
German immigrants who had made it all possible.

Viewing Our Interior Landscape

The German immigrants who settled the Starkenburg area knew great suffering. They were in a
new environment with new customs and a new
language, and they faced the challenges of having
to reconfigure their homes and lives from scratch.
As farmers, they were at the mercy of the weather,
and the weather in the Midwest can be absolutely
brutal. There were none of today's modern con-
veniences in the 1800s. Illness, disease, and death
were as much a part of their lives as farrowing,
planting, and harvesting their crops. Had they left

loved ones behind back in Germany? That, too, could have caused sadness and suffering. And so, they turned to Our Lady of Sorrows for help.

What about you? What sorrows do you bear? What suffering do you carry on your shoulders? Sometimes it can seem as though you're alone in your sadness, as if you are out in the wilderness feeling powerless and wondering how to survive. Our Lady of Sorrows knows all that you're going through. In fact, she knows all that you've been through and all that lies ahead for you. She isn't a disinterested bystander but rather a loving mother who feels your pain and wants to draw you close to her heart so that she can ease that pain. She's there, and she knows what it's like to suffer unspeakable sorrows. All you need do is surrender yourself and your troubles into her tender care, and she will help you.

The Journey Begins

Offer yourself, your loved ones, and our country to Mary, asking her intercession that an appreciation for the richness of our heritage may fill your heart and the hearts of all the people of the United States. Then consecrate yourself and our nation to the Blessed Virgin Mary.

My Queen, My Mother,

I give myself entirely to you. And to show my devotion to you, I consecrate to you this day, my eyes, my ears, my mouth, my heart, my entire self without reserve. As I am your own, my good Mother, guard me and defend me as your property and possession. Amen.

Pray the Rosary for those who sorrow deeply and don't know where to turn. Pray that they will find comfort in Our Lady of Sorrows. Pray also for the leaders of our country that they may guide our nation with wisdom and godly principles.

Stepping Out in Faith

- Are there parts of your cultural heritage your family has held onto? How do they influence your family, your community, and your faith?

- Have you ever felt a sorrow that you didn't know how to handle? What was that like?

- Did you reach out to someone for help? Who? If not, why not?

- How can you reach out to Our Lady of Sorrows today, offering that sorrow or a more recent one?

Basilica and National Shrine of Our Lady of Consolation

CAREY, OHIO

Many notable medical discoveries have been made in the United States. For example, in 1799, Harvard medical professor Benjamin Waterhouse was the first to test the smallpox vaccine,[1] and in 1841, American surgeon Dr. Crawford W. Long performed the first operation using diethyl ether as an anesthetic.[2] In 1922, Elliot Joslin, founder of the Joslin Diabetes Center, introduced insulin as a therapy for treating diabetes.[3] The first successful kidney transplant occurred in 1952 at the Peter

Bent Brigham School of Nursing.[4] In 1958, cardiologist Dr. Seymour Furman extended a patient's life by two months with the first heart pacemaker, and in 1978, Dr. Raymond V. Damadian patented magnetic resonance imaging (MRI) after having used the images to distinguish between normal and cancerous tissue.[5]

These are just a sampling of the long list of groundbreaking medical advancements discovered and implemented by US physicians and researchers. Even at this writing, medical professionals in our country work tirelessly in searching for new ways to diagnose, treat, and cure afflictions that threaten our ability to live long, healthy, and productive lives. The United States has contributed greatly to medical advancement over the centuries and promises to continue to do so into the distant future.

Within our borders, we have countless individuals, organizations, and institutions dedicated to the alleviation of suffering at home and abroad. While news headlines may at times seem to indicate otherwise, there is an endless array of selfless, compassionate people in this country who care deeply about the welfare of others. In many ways, consolation is at the center of the American heart.

Signs from the Pilgrim's Path

Consolation is a recurring theme that winds its way through the history of our country and, likely, through the history of every family who has made their home here. From physical ailments to material, spiritual, and emotional woes, we all are in need of consolation from time to time. I had this on my heart as I visited the Basilica and National Shrine of Our Lady of Consolation in Carey, Ohio.

The village of Carey, with a population of just above 3,500 residents, lies in the northwest part of the state and was founded in 1843 on a donated eighty-acre parcel of land. It's named after John Carey, a prominent businessman who later became a member of the Ohio General Assembly and the US House of Representatives. Carey advocated the building of a railroad that would run between Lake Erie and the Ohio River. Thanks to Carey's foresight, the Mad River and Lake Erie Railroad became the first railroad charter west of the Allegheny Mountains. Eventually, the railroad line passed through the center of Carey, and John Carey became its first president. In time, other railroads were added, and Carey became a busy railroad town. The old depot marking the former location of the tracks is now used as Carey's senior citizen center.[6]

The first half of the nineteenth century saw an influx of immigrants to the United States from Europe, among them families and individuals from the Grand Duchy of Luxembourg. They settled in Wisconsin, Iowa, and the northwestern part of Ohio, and they brought with them a deep devotion to the Blessed Virgin Mary under the title "Mary, Consoler of the Afflicted," whom they had proclaimed the patroness of Luxembourg. Even today, an ancient wooden statue of Mary, Consoler of the Afflicted is the most prominent image in the Cathedral of Luxembourg; the statue's origin is unknown.[7]

Along with the settlers came priests to establish parishes, catechize, and administer the sacraments. In 1868, Fr. Edward Vattman was directed by Bishop Amadeus Rapp to organize a Catholic congregation in Carey and was further instructed to build a church there on land donated by the bishop. Construction on the small chapel named after Fr. Vattman's patron saint, St. Edward, was begun later that year. The year 1873 brought change when Fr. Joseph Peter Gloden was made pastor of St. Edward's with its yet-unfinished church and a congregation of thirteen discouraged families. Refusing a salary so that the funds could be used for building, Fr. Gloden worked alongside his parishioners to complete the work on the church. With new hope, the congregation received permission from the bishop to change the name from St. Edward's to the Church of Our Lady of Consolation. This fulfilled a promise Fr. Gloden had once made to Mary: that he would dedicate to Our Lady of Consolation the first church he would build after his ordination. The church was dedicated on October 18, 1874.[8]

But the parishioners of the Church of Our Lady of Consolation wanted more for our dear Blessed Mother. With Fr. Gloden's inspiration, they decided to procure a replica of the statue of Mary, Consoler of the Afflicted in the Luxembourg cathedral. It was discovered that a member of a neighboring parish was soon to visit his relatives in Luxembourg, and Fr. Gloden asked him to bring the replica statue back with him. Fr. Gloden arranged to have the statue made in Luxembourg and prepared for travel back to Carey. It was carefully formed and crafted in oak to be as similar as possible to the original. It also was made in such a way that it could be clothed just as the original—a time-honored Luxembourgian custom that dates back to the Middle Ages. Precious cloth was used to wrap relics or statues as a form of offering—the exquisite cloth that adorned the sacred image could not be used for other things and was given in thanksgiving for favors granted or in petition. Just like the original statue of Our Lady of Consolation, the replica in Carey was beautifully dressed and adorned with jewels.[9]

A solemn procession took place on May 24, 1875 (Feast of Mary, Helper of Christians) to carry the precious statue from the neighboring parish to the Church of Our Lady of Consolation. News of the event spread quickly, and more than a thousand people gathered for the procession—quite a large number considering that the population of Carey and the surrounding area at that time was mostly Protestant and antagonistic toward Catholics! There was a young man named Leo along the procession route. Leo was an immigrant farmer from Belgium who had four children. His youngest child, Eugenie, had been seriously ill for quite some time. She hadn't been able to retain food for weeks, and her doctor had given up hope of her ever becoming well again. As the statue passed by, Leo fell to his knees and begged Mary, Consoler of the Afflicted to cure his daughter, who lay in bed at home. Upon returning home after the statue's installation, Leo discovered Eugenie sitting at the kitchen table and eating. She'd been completely cured![10]

That's not all. During the week leading up to the procession, violent storms raged over northwest Ohio with strong winds, thunder, and lightning. Gradually, the storm calmed, but a heavy rain continued to pour down that continued all through the night. Undaunted, the people set out in procession with the statue in a covered surrey to protect it. The moment the statue was brought out of the church, the sun broke through the clouds and shone on the line of the procession beginning about a mile from Carey. Yet the rain, thunder, and lightning continued on both sides of it! As soon as the statue was inside the church, there was a sudden cloudburst and the rain poured down once again. The persons processing had hardly enough time to scoot into the church for cover. This miracle had a huge impact on Catholics and Protestants alike and attracted visitors from near and far.[11]

Devotion to Mary, Consoler of the Afflicted increased rapidly, and in 1878, a Confraternity of Our Lady of Consolation was established by special decree of Pope Leo XIII and was accompanied by a gift of a richly embroidered altar frontal and altar cloth. As the number of pilgrims grew, so did the need for updates and expansions to the church and property. A church cemetery was added, a rectory built, and the church steeple replaced after being destroyed by a cyclone in 1896. Soon it became clear that a new, larger church would be needed to accommodate the flow of pilgrims and growing number of parishioners. In 1900, the small chapel was moved to a new location a block away to make room for the new church, and a hall was built as a place for shelter and meals. Ground was broken for the new church in 1907; the corner-stone was blessed in 1919, and construction slowly progressed.[12]

In 1912, the church and property of Our Lady of Consolation came under the administration of the Conventual Franciscan Friars. In 1917, a pilgrim house, or hospice facility, was built for ailing pilgrims and staffed by the Sisters of St. Francis of Tiffin, Ohio. After years of financial and physical setbacks, the new church was finally consecrated on Sunday, June 25, 1925. The statue of Mary, Consoler of the Afflicted was moved from the old chapel to a side altar of the new church, becoming the Shrine of Our Lady of Consolation. Eleven of the members of the original procession on May 24, 1875, were present for the exciting celebration.[13]

In the decades following, an elementary school and a visitor center, cafeteria, and gift shop were constructed. Thirty acres of land were purchased at the end of the road and used to construct Shrine

Park, which features an imported stone altar with a forty-five-foot dome. A twelve-foot, two-ton bronze statue of Our Lady of Consolation rests atop the towering dome. Beautiful, tranquil gardens were added to the park as well as in other areas of the shrine property. In 1971, the Church of Our Lady of Consolation was raised to the rank of a minor basilica by Pope Paul VI. The changing needs of the pilgrims prompted the conversion of the pilgrim house into a retreat house for the shrine's active retreat ministry in the 1990s and was placed in the care of the Franciscan Friars. Today, groups from all over the country come to Our Lady of Consolation for retreat and respite. Visitors from all walks of life and backgrounds come to spend time on the peaceful grounds.[14]

Mostly, however, they come to seek consolation from Mary, Consoler of the Afflicted, in whose arms they find comfort and hope. Since the shrine's inception, countless miracles have occurred at the intercession of Our Lady of Consolation. Although the miracles are well known anecdotally, the shrine administration intentionally does not document them, in keeping with Fr. Gloden's vision to leave everything "to God and to the Blessed Virgin."[15] If there's any proof to be had, it can be found in the glass cases and racks that line the wall of the shrine's lower church. They're filled with casts, crutches, braces, eyeglasses, medical documents, liquor bottles, photos, and personal articles of all kinds from those who have prayed at the shrine and experienced miraculous healings or transformations. There's even an age-old wicker stretcher left behind by a man who was completely cured of paralysis when brought to the shrine.[16] Seeing all of these items brought tears to my eyes—particularly a pair of infant-sized pink eyeglasses—as I imagined the strife caused by the afflictions and the suffering pilgrims' joy and astonishment at being cured.

Fittingly, across the pews from these cases is the Chapel of the Holy Relics, containing more than four hundred relics of saints and blesseds from throughout the centuries. I sat there for a long time, reading through the list of relics all meticulously cataloged. I found the patron saints of every member of my family and prayed for them there, each by name. Then I thanked these heroic men and women for their faithful example of love for Christ and his Mother.

In the back of the lower church is a long glass case containing all of the outfits for Our Lady of Consolation that have been given by pilgrims since the shrine's early days, including the dress she wore in the May 24, 1875, procession! Judging by the number of hangers and the space occupied, I estimated that there must be at least 500! A member of the shrine's staff told me that the dresses have all been handmade of luxurious fabric and costly ornamentation. They were marvelous! The outfits are changed about every two weeks throughout the year and for special feast days and celebrations. As I stood there, gazing at all the gorgeous gowns, I smiled and murmured, "Our Blessed Mother is the best-dressed woman in the world!" Rightfully so, for she is the Queen of Heaven.

I saved the best for last—the Shrine of Our Lady of Consolation in the upper basilica. Having taken in the rest of the property, I wanted to sit silently before Mary, Consoler of the Afflicted undistracted and ready to absorb whatever it might be that she would say to me. I was not disappointed. For as full as my heart already was from all I'd experienced that day, she filled it even more. Our Lady had been at this place for 150 years, consoling, encouraging, interceding, curing, and loving her children. She came to a tiny Midwest railroad town at the request of a holy country priest from Luxembourg to a people who longed for the consolation she had to offer. I thought of the shrine's complicated history and the long list of people involved. So much had gone into making this place what it is today!

I allowed my eyes to linger on the statue. Mary holds our Lord tenderly in her left arm, and with her right hand she holds a golden scepter. A jeweled heart and a golden key hang from her right arm—a representation of the key Napoleon is said to have given her when he and his troops invaded the Grand Duchy of Luxembourg. Our Lady and her Son both wear ornate crowns, symbolic of their roles in the headship in the Church.[17] I studied the beautiful gown and veil she wore that day and wondered what miracle she had granted to the pilgrim who had made it for her. What kind of affliction had he or she suffered? How did our Lady answer that person's pleas for consolation? The magnificence of the statue with its symbols, jewels, and fabrics was for me a reflection of the consoling power the heavenly Father had bestowed on the precious jewel who became the Mother of his Son.

Viewing Our Interior Landscape

Consolation is indeed at the center of the American heart. Compassion moves us to relieve the affliction of others, but at the same time, we long to have relief for our own afflictions. We work diligently on a practical level toward this—too much sometimes. When we work hard to rid others of suffering or to be rid of our own suffering, we can get so wrapped up in the process and drive to succeed that we forget what, or rather Who, is the real source of consolation: God. This is why science oftentimes moves dangerously close to the limit of morality. Just because we can doesn't mean we should, and so research and development can go in ungodly directions. We're called to console the afflicted, but we must take care to find ways to console that are benevolent, according to natural law, and follow God's holy will. In this we can and should look to our Mother Mary for example and guidance. She is Our Lady of Consolation and wants nothing more than our happiness and sanctification, even when the path of consolation requires things that are very difficult for us to bear.

What about you? Are you in need of consolation right now? Perhaps your affliction is physical, such as a chronic or incurable disease or an injury. Perhaps you're facing a spiritual crisis, and your faith is waning. It could be that you're overwhelmed by financial concerns, problems at work, or difficulties in a relationship. These are all forms of affliction for which you need consolation. You don't have to suffer alone. In fact, you're not suffering alone even if it might seem that way. There is someone who suffers with you, who knows every corner of your heart, how you suffer, what you need, and the best way to console you. Our Lady of Consolation knows you better than you know yourself, and she knows exactly what you need to get through this. Because of her closeness to her Son—the One who suffered, died, and rose again for you—Mary has the right and power to intercede in all your afflictions. She is waiting to offer you consolation. You need only open your afflicted heart to her.

The Journey Begins

Offer yourself, your loved ones, and our country to Mary, asking her intercession and guidance in all our afflictions. Then consecrate yourself and our nation to the Blessed Virgin Mary.

My Queen, My Mother,

I give myself entirely to you. And to show my devotion to you, I consecrate to you this day, my eyes, my ears, my mouth, my heart, my entire self without reserve. As I am your own, my good Mother, guard me and defend me as your property and possession. Amen.

Pray the Rosary for those who have fallen into pride and divisiveness. Pray also for the leaders of our country that they may guide our nation with wisdom and godly principles.

Stepping Out in Faith

- How has your heart been touched by the story of Our Lady of Consolation?

- What afflictions do you face right now?

- What makes them hard for you to bear?

- If you were to design a gown for Our Lady of Consolation, what would it look like? Why would you give it to her?

The National Shrine of Our Lady of Good Help

CHAMPION, WISCONSIN

Each year, the Sanctuary of Our Lady of Lourdes attracts more than six million visitors.[1] More than five million visitors pilgrimage to the Sanctuary of Fatima annually.[2] Why do they go? They go because they want to see the places where the Blessed Virgin Mary appeared. In 1858, Our Lady appeared to Bernadette Soubirous in a cave in Lourdes, France, as she was gathering firewood for her family. In 1917, Our Lady appeared to three shepherd children—Lucia, Jacinta, and Francisco—in a cove near the place they were shepherding their sheep in Fatima, Portugal. The cave in Lourdes and the cove, which has now been made into a grotto, in Fatima are still there and are still holy places from which our Mother Mary distributes graces.

While the United States does not boast of a shrine as large as either Lourdes or Fatima, there are many smaller places throughout the world, sites where Our Lady appeared with a special message and mission for her children. She wants to be present to us in very real ways and to guide us toward her Son for the sake of our salvation. She wants to be present to us here, in these United States of America, and she wants us to know that she is our Mother, who cares for us as no human mother ever could.

Signs from the Pilgrim's Path

The most striking thing about the Shrine of Our Lady of Good Help in Champion, Wisconsin, is its simplicity. Tucked away in a rural area of the Diocese of Green Bay, the shrine is surrounded by farms. Unless you were looking for it, you wouldn't know it was there. That was the case for a very long time until, on December 8, 2010, Green Bay bishop David Ricken officially approved the Marian apparitions that took place there, making it the first and only Church-approved Marian apparition site in the United States. Now, a steady stream of pilgrims from all over the world visit the shrine.

The National Shrine of Our Lady of Good Help rests on six acres of land where, in 1859, Mary appeared to a twenty-four-year-old woman named Adele Brice.[3] Adele immigrated to Wisconsin with her parents and three siblings in 1855 to join the Belgian community of Bay Settlement. Pioneer life was difficult, and everyone in the family was required to pitch in working in the fields with primitive tools, planting, harvesting, and carrying sacks of grain on their heads to the grist mill—a distance of many miles.[4] The first apparition occurred while Adele was on her way to the grist mill. Along the path, she saw a lady standing between two trees—a maple and a hemlock—dressed all in white and with a yellow sash around her waist. Frightened, Adele stood still. The vision slowly disappeared, leaving a white cloud after it. When she told her parents about it, they surmised that it was a poor soul in need of prayers.[5]

On the following Sunday, October 9, Adele passed the same spot on her way to Mass in Bay Settlement, eleven miles away from her home and accompanied by one of her sisters and a neighbor

woman. When they neared the maple and hemlock
trees, the lady in white appeared again, stayed for
a few moments and disappeared, leaving a white
cloud behind. Although the other two had not
seen the lady, they knew something had frightened Adele. Upon reaching Bay Settlement, Adele
consulted her spiritual director, who advised her
that if the lady appeared again, she should ask,
"In God's name, who are you, and what do you
want of me?" He assured her that if the apparition
was a heavenly messenger, it would not harm her.
Adele returned home, accompanied by her two
companions and a man who was clearing land for
the Holy Cross fathers at Bay Settlement. As they
approached the area of the trees, Adele saw the
beautiful lady clothed in dazzling white, with a
yellow sash around her waist. She wore a crown
of stars around her head and her long, golden,
wavy hair fell loosely over her shoulders. A heavenly light shone around her so brightly that Adele
could hardly look at her face. Overcome, Adele fell
on her knees.

"In God's name, who are you, and what do
you want of me?" Adele asked.

"I am the Queen of Heaven who prays for
the conversion of sinners, and I wish you to do
the same. You received Holy Communion this

morning and that is well. But you must do more. Make a general confession and offer Communion for the conversion of sinners. If they do not convert and do penance, my Son will be obliged to punish them," our Lady said.

Adele's companions, weeping, asked her who was there and why they were unable to see it.

"Kneel," said Adele, "The Lady says she is the Queen of Heaven."

At that moment our Lady turned and looked kindly at them, saying, "Blessed are they that believe without seeing."

"What are you doing here in idleness," continued our Lady to Adele, "while your companions are working in the vineyard of my Son?"

"What more can I do, dear Lady?" Adele asked, weeping.

"Gather the children in this wild country and teach them what they should know for salvation," she answered.

"But how shall I teach them who knows so little myself?" replied Adele.

"Teach them," replied our Lady, "their catechism, how to sign themselves with the Sign of the Cross, and how to approach the sacraments; that is what I wish you to do. Go, and fear nothing; I will help you."

Enveloped in that radiant light, our Lady lifted her hands as though she were beseeching a blessing for those present. Slowly, she vanished from sight leaving Adele overwhelmed and prostrate on the ground.

The people of the Bay Settlement area were astounded at Adele's account of what had happened that day. Most of them believed it, but some questioned Adele's mental stability.[6] Adele took the Queen of Heaven's words seriously and, from then on, committed herself to this mission she had received, traveling a fifty-mile radius on foot, teaching the faith door-to-door, staying with a family a night or two, and then moving on to the next house perhaps miles away.[7]

Immediately after the apparitions, Adele's father built a small log oratory on the site. By 1861, pilgrims were arriving almost daily to see the privileged place, so the settlers built a larger chapel over the ground on which the maple and hemlock trees grew, placing the main altar exactly above the trees' location.

Adele eventually formed a community of women dedicated to teaching children the faith, called the Sisters of Good Health.[8] They established a convent and children's boarding school, frame structures that were built between 1865 and

1868, and in 1869, the school was officially named St. Mary's Academy.[9] The Sisters of Good Help and their work were supported solely by donations. They refused no one, and soon parents who no longer could care for their children were leaving them on the sisters' doorstep, never to return. It was not uncommon for them to run completely out of food for themselves and the children. When this happened, Sr. Adele would offer words of encouragement to her fellow sisters and spend the night in prayer. The next morning they would find a basket of food outside the door or some kind person would show up with a delivery of goods.[10]

Other miracles were granted by Sr. Adele's prayers, the most notable of which took place in 1871. On October 8—the same night as the Great Chicago Fire—the drought-stricken town of Peshtigo, Wisconsin, caught fire, scorching 1.2 million acres and killing 800 people.[11] As the flames roared toward them, the people of Champion, Wisconsin, fled, seeking refuge in the chapel of Our Lady of Good Help. Sr. Adele led them in a Rosary procession around the building and then brought them inside for protection; they prayed through the night. In the morning, the entire grounds and buildings had been miraculously preserved from the flames, which swept over the chapel, school, and land without causing so much as a cinder. The foliage on the property was left lush and green, and the fence posts surrounding the property were singed on the outside while left perfectly unscathed on the side facing toward the chapel.[12]

In 1880, the wooden chapel was razed and a brick one erected in its place, followed by a brick convent and school in 1885. The Sisters of Good Health carried on Sr. Adele's work for several years after her death in 1896, eventually turning it over to the Sisters of St. Francis of Bay Settlement. St. Mary's Academy closed in 1928 and was converted into a home for handicapped children in 1933.[13]

In 1942, a fourth chapel—the one currently standing—was built and was dedicated by Bishop Paul Rhode under the title "Our Lady of Good Help." During construction of the new chapel, excavators discovered the stumps of the maple and hemlock trees between which Mary had appeared; they had long been forgotten, along with the fact that the main altar had been placed directly above them. The stumps were preserved and a crypt built in their place, just below the current main altar of the shrine in a cozy basement chapel. In 1953, the school was converted into a pre-novitiate for the

Sisters of St. Francis whose motherhouse was in Bay Settlement.[14]

Today, the brick buildings stand as testament to the courage and fortitude of Sr. Adele. A caretaker lives in a small house just a few yards from the school building, and a gift shop has been added for visitors. The shrine has come under the authority of the Diocese of Green Bay, and it is administered by the Fathers of Mercy. On the grounds behind the buildings there is an outdoor Stations of the Cross and a Joyful Mysteries of the Rosary walkway for private or group meditation. In the summer, the grounds bloom with flowers and decorative plants. Next to the crypt entrance lies the chapel cemetery, where Sr. Adele and two of her fellow Sisters of Good Health are buried, along with a few settlers and benefactors. Within the shrine itself, the center of attention is the statue of our Lady above the luminous tabernacle on the main altar. Embedded in the left wall is a lighted glass case that holds a smaller statue of Mary as the Queen of Heaven; this statue is used in the shrine's annual Feast of the Assumption procession that has been held every August 15 since Sr. Adele's time. Beneath the statue is a reliquary that houses two small pieces of wood: one from each of the two trees between which the Blessed Mother appeared to Sr. Adele. Beside that is a smaller reliquary containing a tiny swatch from the Blessed Mother's veil. This is an ancient relic, not from the apparition.

The real attraction is the crypt beneath the shrine. A statue of Mary stands between two adoring angels, illumined by spotlights and racks of votive candles: a reminder of the intentions of those seeking her intercession. With room for no more than about twenty people, the crypt offers space to quietly reflect on the miracle that took place there in 1859. It has a certain feel to it, not in the physical sense but in the spiritual sense. I've been to the shrine many times, and I experience the same thing on every visit. Upon entering, an all-consuming calm suddenly washes over me. It's as if nothing else in the world matters except my being there, and I become overwhelmed by the presence of Mary.

Throughout history, Mary has appeared in specific times and places in response to current events and with a message that is to be carried into the future. The apparitions of Our Lady of Good Help are no different. The North Woods of Wisconsin were wilderness, with the sparse population spread out and few priests to cover an expansive territory. The settlers there were meagerly educated, including about Catholicism, and had brought with them old-world customs that were incompatible with Catholic teachings, causing a watering down of the faith and a laxity in its practice. The children weren't being taught their catechism and there was danger of the Catholic faith disappearing entirely. Our Lady's poignant message to Adele hit the proverbial nail on the head. Someone—Adele—must turn the tide immediately for that generation and those to come. And because of Adele's actions, faith flourished rather than disappeared.

Viewing Our Interior Landscape

Adele was just a young, barely educated woman when the Queen of Heaven appeared to her. She was overwhelmed by the apparition and even more so by the magnitude of the task given to her. "But how shall I teach them who knows so little myself?" she asked our Lady. Clearly, she felt as though she was underprepared and underqualified. It was only after Mary promised her help that Adele had the courage to proceed with her mission.

Have you ever been overwhelmed and felt as though you were underprepared and underqualified for the task given you? Have you ever questioned yourself when faced with certain responsibilities? Did you have the inclination to beg off because of your doubts? You're not the only one to experience this; many, if not most, of us have. In such situations, there's one vital question you must ask yourself: *Is this God's will for me?* If it is indeed God's will, then you'll be given the grace, courage, and know-how to carry out your mission. What's more, if you invoke Our Lady of Good Help, she'll see you through it.

The Journey Begins

Offer yourself, your loved ones, and our country to Mary, asking her intercession that your heart and the hearts of all the people of the United States may be open to her message for our times. Then, consecrate yourself and our nation to Mary.

My Queen, My Mother,

I give myself entirely to you. And to show my devotion to you, I consecrate to you this day, my eyes, my ears, my mouth, my heart, my entire self without reserve. As I am your own, my good Mother, guard me and defend me as your property and possession. Amen.

Pray the Rosary for those who have closed their hearts to our Blessed Mother and her Son. Pray also for the leaders of our country that they may guide our nation with wisdom and godly principles,

Stepping Out in Faith

- How much do you know about Marian apparitions and their meaning? How can you learn more?

- How would you describe your relationship with Mary? What can you do to deepen it?

- Why do you think Mary appeared in Champion, Wisconsin? How does that affect you?

Shrine of Our Lady of Martyrs

AURIESVILLE, NEW YORK

Every Memorial Day, we pause to remember those who have fallen in the line of duty while fighting to defend our freedoms here in the United States. Memorial Day is a federal holiday, celebrated annually on the last Monday of May. Special services are held in veterans' cemeteries throughout the nation, honoring the brave men and women who gave their lives for us. It's a time to remember, pray, and give thanks. There are others who have died for us as well, others who also suffered terribly at the hands of hostile forces, who made the ultimate sacrifice so that Christianity would take root and thrive throughout this great nation. The former suffered and died so that we could practice our faith. The latter suffered and died to bring it here in the first place. Most of the former shed their blood on foreign soil. The latter shed their blood on North American soil.

Signs from the Pilgrim's Path

I had read long ago about the North American martyrs, about their bravery and the horrible tortures they endured while struggling to bring Catholicism to the New World. However, I shied away from the gory details because I feared that the impression they would leave on me would profoundly disturb my peace. That was my loss. When I prepared for my visit to the Shrine of Our Lady of Martyrs in Auriesville, New York, I went back to those stories and allowed myself to take in the details. For the other shrines of Marian pilgrimage, I refrained from studying too much ahead of time because I didn't want any preconceived notions to alter my impressions. This shrine was my one and only exception, and I'm grateful I made that decision because it added depth to my visit. It's one thing to read about martyrs. It's another thing to walk the ground upon which they shed their blood.

The Shrine of Our Lady of Martyrs is built on the site of what once was the Mohawk village of Ossernenon. It marks the place of martyrdom of three of the eight North American martyrs: Fr. Isaac Jogues and his two lay companions, René Goupil and John LaLande. They were martyred in the 1640s, along with five Jesuit priests martyred in Canada. Ossernenon is also believed to be the 1656 birthplace of St. Kateri Tekakwitha.[1]

The Jesuits came to America via Canada in the early 1600s, with the intention of converting the Native Americans to Christianity. The greatest danger they faced were the fearsome Iroquois, which were a federation of the Mohawk, Oneida, Onondaga, Cayuga, and Seneca tribes. This federation showed no mercy to their enemies and exterminated any tribe that would not submit to their dominance. The Iroquois were at war with the Hurons and Algonquins, two tribes allied with the French. The growing influence of the French around the Great Lakes infuriated the Iroquois, which also turned them against the Hurons and Algonquins. As you can imagine, the French missionary Jesuits were not welcome by the Iroquois, nor was the God that they brought with them.[2]

The first French Jesuits to come to Canada
were led by Fr. John de Brebeuf, arriving in 1625.
The Jesuit's plan for evangelization was for a missionary to set out with one or two companions,
travel into the heart of the wilderness, and live
among the Native Americans with the intent to
convert them one soul at a time. They studied and
became fluent in the native language and learned
the religious customs of the tribe. Then they par-
alleled the Native Americans beliefs with those
of the Gospel, and in this way, the tribes were
gradually won for Christ.[3] Fr. Brebeuf and his
companions traveled the regions of Lake Huron
to evangelize the Huron tribe. In 1636, Fr. Isaac
Jogues joined him. In 1642, Fr. Jogues embarked on
an 800-mile journey along the French, Ottawa, and
St. Lawrence rivers toward what is now New York
state. With frequent Iroquois raids along the St.
Lawrence, the trip was dangerous on many levels.[4]

While traveling, Fr. Jogues met René Goupil,
who aspired to become a Jesuit priest but was held
back by his deafness. He instead became a lay
Jesuit and served in his capacity as physician and
surgeon to those in need. Another Jesuit layman,
William Couture, and a young Catholic Huron girl
named Theresa accompanied them. They were
ambushed and attacked by Iroquois as they drew

close to shore. In all, the Iroquois captured twenty-two party members and killed another eighteen. Over a two-week period, the captives were taken by canoe and on foot to the Mohawk valley miles away, stopping at various Iroquois villages along the way where they were further brutalized. In the interim, Goupil asked to profess his vows. Fr. Jogues accepted his request and blessed him as a brother in the Society of Jesus.[5]

The suffering they endured is unspeakable—including running the gauntlet, burning, torture, mutilation, and more. The prisoners were split into small groups and sent to various villages. There the villagers would routinely strip the prisoners naked, club them, gnaw their fingers and hands to a pulp, burn their flesh with lighted torches, toss hot coals on their exposed bodies, pull out their hair and beards by the roots, reopen their wounds, and more. Several of Fr. Jogues's fingers were severed, including his index fingers and thumbs—those used by the priest to hold the consecrated Host at Mass. Fr. Jogues and his companions somehow survived the ordeal.[6]

One day, Goupil was caught making the Sign of the Cross over a Mohawk child. Some accounts say that he was caught baptizing him. Goupil's actions angered the boy's grandfather, who was suspicious and thought Goupil might be casting an evil spell on the boy. The grandfather, an elder of the village, ordered Goupil's death, and so his braves waited patiently for the opportune moment. Days later, as Goupil and Fr. Jogues prayed the Rosary together—the first recitation of the Rosary documented in what would become New York state—the opportune moment came. As they finished praying, a Mohawk brave approached Goupil and split his skull with a tomahawk.[7]

His body was dumped into a nearby ravine, where it was prey to wild animals. Fr. Jogues, grief-stricken over the loss of his dear friend, waited until nightfall to search for the body so that he could bury it. He was not immediately success-ful, but eventually he found Goupil's ravaged body and used rocks to submerge it in a nearby creek for later burial. Heartbreakingly, the body was no longer there when Fr. Jogues returned to bury it because flooding had carried it away. The next spring, Fr. Jogues was able to find Goupil's skull and a few of his bones and buried them in the ravine, but Goupil's exact burial spot has never been discovered. The Catholic Church teaches that those who are murdered for the faith can be considered martyrs and have the potential to be named saints. Furthermore, the physical remains of a saint are considered first class relics and worthy of veneration. Since Goupil's remains are still buried in the ravine, the entire ravine is now a reliquary of his remains and worthy of veneration.[8]

Fr. Jogues continued on as a Mohawk prisoner until, in 1643, he was discovered by the Dutch who convinced him to allow them to rescue him. Perhaps it seems strange that there would be any convincing to do, but even in captivity and with all of the tortures he endured, Fr. Jogues still was dedicated to the conversion of the Mohawks. With the help of the Dutch, Fr. Jogues escaped his captors and returned to France where he was zealously welcomed and treated with great respect and honor. He received proper clothing, nutritious meals, and medical treatment for his torn and weakened body. He was again united with his Jesuit community and able to visit with family and friends who had missed him and whom he had missed. But the Hurons never left his mind and heart. Still passionate for their conversion, he adamantly requested that his superiors allow him to return to Canada. Permission was granted, and four months later Fr. Jogues again stepped onto the Canadian shore, where he learned that the French government had appointed him as their peace ambassador to the Iroquois! Two years later,

Fr. Jogues proceeded to Ossernenon, the village where he had been kept as a prisoner, this time accompanied by another lay Jesuit, John LaLande.

Initially, the situation worked favorably for Fr. Jogues, and he was able to negotiate peace between the French and the Iroquois. After some time, Fr. Jogues had to return to Quebec to report to the French government officials there. In his haste, he left behind a chest containing some religious articles. During the same time, a devastating plague swept through the Mohawk Valley, wiping out a large part of the population. The tribe's medicine men blamed the black box that Fr. Jogues had left behind and threw it in to the river. Bitter hatred brewed in their hearts for this man who, they believed, had caused the plague. Meanwhile, back in Quebec, the missionaries had decided to open a mission to the Mohawks in Ossernenon. On the way back, they were captured, and the Mohawk chiefs contemplated their fate, knowing that the missionaries had the backing of the French government. As the chiefs were meeting, an angry Mohawk brave decided their fate for himself and invited Fr. Jogues to a banquet, presumably with the purpose of making peace. As the priest entered the cabin, the brave wielded his tomahawk and split open his skull. John LaLande met the same fate days later as he was searching for his companion's body. Their heads were placed on the village palisades as a warning to the French.[9]

So ended the lives of Fr. Jogues, René Goupil, and John LaLande, killed viciously as they courageously tried to bring the Catholic faith to the land that is now the United States of America.

The Shrine of Our Lady of Martyrs was founded in 1884 by Jesuit Fr. Joseph Loyzance on a ten-acre plot of land with a simple structure dedicated to Our Lady of Martyrs. The current shrine was built in 1930 and in the shape of a coliseum—the first circular church in the United States. Seating 6,000, it's open from early April to October 19 (the feast day of the North American martyrs) for visitors, weekly Masses, and a wide range of special religious events and celebrations. Today, the land spans 600 acres and includes Stations of the Cross, meditation gardens and chapels for prayer, facilities for groups, and an outstanding museum.[10]

The grounds are both ominous and glorious. Mohawk longhouses and the platforms on which prisoners were shamed, burned, and mutilated once stood there. One can look down the steep hill descending to the Mohawk River—the same hill that Fr. Jogues and René Goupil, already beaten, maimed, and weakened, were made to ascend through a gauntlet of enraged, armed Mohawk warriors. Reverence, sadness, awe, and gratitude filled my heart. I prayed that, if faced with the same circumstances, I would be as courageous.

Across the road is the ravine where Fr. Jogues buried René Goupil's remains. The paved pathway leading down the hill is lined with placards telling Goupil's incredible story. Each step leads one's heart deeper into the reality of this man's astounding sacrifice for the faith. More pathways wind through and around the ravine, along which are statues and places of devotion, including a lovely outdoor Marian shrine at its center. There is silence but for the muffled footsteps of pilgrims prayerfully wandering the sacred ground that has been soaked with the blood of martyrs. I stayed in the ravine for good part of the afternoon in awe. Over and over, the tears flowed down my cheeks as I realized the significance of the land upon which I stood. The ground itself commanded reverence, and that reverence poured out of my heart. I tried to pray, but I couldn't—not anything intelligible, that is. The only thing that came from my lips was, "Thank you," repeated until my throat became dry. I was indeed treading on ground that has been soaked with the blood of martyrs.

Viewing Our Interior Landscape

When someone mentions martyrdom, what comes your mind? Perhaps most people think of the Christians of the early Church who were ravaged by wild beasts in the Coliseum, beheaded, crucified, and tortured in any number of ways because they would not renounce Jesus Christ. There are others martyred for the faith in different centuries and areas of the world such as in Japan, Mexico, and even in today's Middle Eastern countries. The North American martyrs were murdered because they tried to spread the faith on this continent. Do you ever stop to consider what this country would be like without their sacrifices? There are numerous forces that threaten the vitality and growth of the Catholic Church in our country today. Perhaps you've encountered some yourself, either directly or indirectly. Perhaps you've already been required to suffer for your faith. If not, there's a good possibility that it will be required of you in the future. Will you be prepared? You can't be absolutely certain how you'd respond; no one can be. But you can be certain that calling on the Holy Spirit and the intercession of the North American martyrs will give you the grace and courage you need.

The Journey Begins

Offer yourself, your loved ones, and our country to Mary, asking her intercession that courageous dedication to our faith fill your heart and the hearts of all the people of the United States. Then, consecrate yourself and our nation to the Blessed Virgin Mary.

> My Queen, My Mother,
>
> I give myself entirely to you. And to show my devotion to you, I consecrate to you this day, my eyes, my ears, my mouth, my heart, my entire self without reserve. As I am your own, my good Mother, guard me and defend me as your property and possession. Amen.

Pray the Rosary for those who lack courage to stand up for the Christian faith and for those who do not believe. Pray also for the leaders of our country that they may guide our nation with wisdom and godly principles.

Stepping Out in Faith

- How is your mind and heart impacted by the story of the North American martyrs?

- Why do you think the shrine was named Our Lady of Martyrs? What significance does Mary have there?

- How can you show your gratitude for the sacrifice of martyrs?

- Does the story of the North American martyrs impact your thoughts and feelings about our country? How?

DAY EIGHT

The House of Mary Shrine

YANKTON, SOUTH DAKOTA

In certain ways, America was built on philanthropy. America's very first philanthropists were the natives of the Bahamas who greeted Columbus when he first set foot in the New World in 1492. They were generous to the explorer and his crew, giving away virtually everything that was asked of them. When the pilgrims at Plymouth grappled with their new environment in 1620, the Native American Squanto offered them wisdom and practical assistance even though he himself had once been kidnapped and carried away by an Englishman and sold into slavery. In the 1700s, many philanthropists used their wealth to build poor houses and hospitals and to fund the Revolutionary War. Among them was Eleazar Wheelock, whose school for Native Americans evolved into Dartmouth College.[1] In the next century, Joseph de Veuster, better known as Fr. Damian, took compassion on the leper colony on the Hawaiian Islands, organized a massive fundraising campaign to improve the lepers' living conditions, and eventually moved into the colony himself in 1873.[2] St. Katharine Drexel, who founded the Sisters of the Blessed Sacrament for Indians and Colored People in 1891, inherited a massive estate when both of her parents died. She spent her fortune on missionary and charity works and eventually founded a network of 145 missions, 12 schools for Native Americans, and 50 schools for African Americans throughout the South and West. In 1915, she founded Xavier University in New Orleans with a $750,000 grant from her fortune.[3]

But it's not only billionaires who have become great American philanthropists; private individuals also give of their time, talents, and resources to do good for our nation. That list could never be completed, since their heroic efforts are seldom catalogued or publicized. And yet, without these contributions—both big and small—the United States would not be the amazing country that it is today.

Signs from the Pilgrim's Path

Ed and Jeanne English, founders of the House of Mary Shrine in Yankton, South Dakota, are among America's great philanthropists.

In 1957, the Englishes obtained a prime 640-acre piece of land near the banks of Lewis and Clark Lake in Yankton. The area around the lake was used primarily for recreational sites, such as campgrounds, resorts, and vacation homes, and the land the Englishes had purchased would be perfect for that. They intended to build their own home there and then develop the rest. However, the couple had a strong Marian devotion, and their first inclination was to pray to Mary and ask her to show them how to use this large parcel of land. The chaplain from Mount Marty College in Yankton was a good friend of theirs, and so Ed and Jeanne invited him to visit and tour the land with them. As they walked, the Englishes pointed out the beauty of the terrain and its easy accessibility to the city of Yankton and to vacationers in the park below. Before departing, the priest gave his friends some advice. He advised them not to sell all of the land but rather to save some of it for "an edifice for God." Ed and Jeanne took his advice to heart. They sold some of the land but kept forty-five acres for God.[4]

They were committed to creating an edifice for God. A group called the Rosary Makers began meeting monthly in the cabin on the property, now known as the Little House of Mary, to pray and make rosaries for worldwide distribution. Soon, they were inspired to erect three giant crosses at the hilltop as reminders of the life and death of Jesus Christ. The Rosary Makers and their volunteers constructed the seventy-foot tall crosses and hauled them up to the top of the hill where they can be seen from the surrounding distance. As each cross was hoisted into place, a miraculous ring appeared around the sun. Three crosses, three miraculous rings. Everyone present witnessed it and took it as an affirmation that God was pleased with their efforts. Before the last ring disappeared, Jeanne English grabbed her camera and snapped a photo. The framed photograph hangs in the St. Joseph Chapel on the property.[5]

The Rosary Makers wanted to do even more. They wanted to build a shrine on the land that would honor Mary. In 1970, they formed a committee that approached the bishop with their desire and he granted them his permission and approval. This delighted the Rosary Makers, yet they worried how it might be accomplished. A Benedictine monk encouraged them. "It will never be easy, but those of you who work on the shrine will be blessed and the area will be blessed," he said.

He was right. Even though there were difficulties, the edifice for God and for Mary began to take shape. The next summer, twelve donors sponsored Stations of the Cross. One warm summer day, each donor carried his or her station up the high hill on a path that wound through wild plum and sumac bushes. Beginning at the bottom and ending near the top, the group erected the stations. After that came a succession of developments. A replica of the tomb of Christ was built on the side of the hill's peak so that those who pray the Stations of the Cross may also experience the joy of the Resurrection. Holy stairs were crafted, leading to a meditation area halfway up the hill, and a specific prayer was assigned to each stair. The prayers were published in *The Holy Stairs Prayer Booklet*, a publication visitors can carry along as they go. Nearby a statue of Moses and an iron creation of St. Michael were placed, both sculpted by a local artist, as well as a replica of the *Pietà*. Behind the hill were erected hermitages—small cabins in a secluded area of the woods that may be used for meditation and quiet retreats. A special entryway, called "Mary's Entrance," was donated by a couple in thanksgiving for a miracle received through Mary's intercession. It includes a large statue of Mary flanked by a series of nine pillars, each depicting a scene in Mary's life and apparitions. In later years, a Rosary pond was added behind Mary's Entrance and fountains were positioned on the incline of the hill.

On the land, there are now three outdoor rosaries—a large, wooden, fifteen-decade rosary winding through the trees, a rosary of roses on the hillside, and one surrounding the Rosary Pond. Funds were raised and a local artist was hired to design a hand-beveled crystal window depicting Mary surrounded by a rosary with the Holy Spirit hovering over her. This window replaced the original one in the Little House of Mary and made it a place for meditation and prayer. A local sculptor crafted and donated a statue of St. Joseph that originally stood on the grounds but was moved to the Little House of Mary in 2009 when the English family donated a marble statue of St. Joseph that stands in its place.

Still, something was missing. The shrine needed a chapel. Local companies volunteered time and materials to dig the basement, lay the bricks, form the structure, and furnish the building. The cross was designed by a Baptist neighbor, and the shrine's first spiritual director donated six hundred dollars. The holy Mass vessels, statuary, altar linens, candle holders, crucifix, tabernacle, monstrance, sanctuary light—virtually all items inside the chapel—were donated by patrons or local churches. Initially, the chapel was heated with a donated wood furnace, which has since been updated. The beautiful little chapel was named the Chapel of St. Joseph.[6]

Even now, the House of Mary volunteers and benefactors continue to develop the land. Recent additions include the Holy Innocents garden and Holy Innocents memorial honoring the unborn. The statue was donated by a woman who had lost a baby at birth and shows Jesus with an unborn child resting in his extended hand. Nearby is Rachel Weeping for Her Children (see Jeremiah 3:15), an expansion of the Holy Innocents memorial. It's dedicated to the memory of all children lost to miscarriage, abortion, or childhood death, and grieving parents leave the names of their lost children at the foot of the statue. The Way of the Saints is a pillar-lined pathway, each pillar adorned with a picture and brief biography of a

saint throughout the centuries—nearly fifty saints
in all. The most recent addition to the property is a
veteran's memorial honoring all who have served
in our Armed Forces.

Words can't adequately describe the House of
Mary Shrine. Without seeing it, one might think it's
a mere hodgepodge of structures. That couldn't be
further from the truth! It's an aesthetically planned
and purposeful array of ways to experience the
glory of God and express love for his Mother Mary.
It's meant to be taken in slowly, gratefully, and on
more than just one visit. Most remarkable is that it
has all been accomplished entirely by volunteers
and donors dedicated to turning a beautiful tract
of land into a place to find peace, grace, and time
with God and our Mother, Mary. The volunteers
and donors present and past are unsung heroes,
modern-day philanthropists who give and have
given freely of their time, talents, and resources
to develop and maintain a resplendent edifice for
God.

Viewing Our Interior Landscape

Have you ever taken stock of all the goods,
resources, talents, and abilities God has given
you? If you listed them one by one, you probably would have quite a long list—longer than you

would have expected to come up with. Have you ever considered why you were give these gifts and what God expects you to do with them? This is the example set by Ed and Jeanne English for all of us in this great land of ours.

Have you ever seen yourself as a philanthropist? You may not be wealthy or have notable possessions, but you do have much to offer, and there is much you can do that will give glory to God. In your own way, in your own place in the world, and within your own environment, you can be a philanthropist by reaching out to others in your day-to-day living. Philanthropy doesn't always have to involve material goods. There is the possibility of being a spiritual philanthropist by giving to others with your prayers, sacrifices, being, and actions. The most wonderful thing about philanthropy, whether material or spiritual, is that it becomes contagious—and our country is in need of a veritable epidemic. If you turn yourself over to God and place yourself into the hands of our Blessed Mother Mary, they will show you how to make your surroundings into an edifice for God.

The Journey Begins

Offer yourself, your loved ones, and our country to Mary, asking her intercession that lasting charity

may fill your heart and hearts of all the people of
the United States. Then consecrate yourself and
our nation to the Blessed Virgin Mary.

> My Queen, My Mother,
>
> I give myself entirely to you. And to show my
> devotion to you, I consecrate to you this day,
> my eyes, my ears, my mouth, my heart, my
> entire self without reserve. As I am your own,
> my good Mother, guard me and defend me as
> your property and possession. Amen.

Pray the Rosary for those who lack charity and
are reticent to extend themselves for the good of
others. Pray also for the leaders of our country that
they may guide our nation with wisdom and godly
principles.

Stepping Out in Faith

- What most impresses you about the House of
  Mary Shrine?

- In what ways might Jesus' Mother, Mary, be
  considered a philanthropist? During her life-
  time on earth? In the time since?

- What can you do to foster greater charity in
  your own heart and in the hearts of others?

- What kind of philanthropist might you
  become?

DAY NINE

Our Lady of Peace Shrine

SANTA CLARA, CALIFORNIA

America is often referred to as "the land of opportunity," and rightfully so. There is opportunity here for anyone who invests in a dream and works hard toward a worthy goal. Our Founding Fathers had a dream to form a new democratic republic that would assure freedom and equality for all. The pioneers had a dream to traverse new territories and forge a better life for themselves and their families. The developers and architects of our country had a dream to build infrastructure and raise great cities that would be centers of commerce and culture. Our nation has been inspired and led by dreams since it began. Dreams are what keep us going; dreams that rest in God's providence are what become reality.

Signs from the Pilgrim's Path

Before I went to California, "Silicon Valley" was just another place I heard about in the media. It wasn't real to me. It became real as I flew into the San Jose airport, giving me an aerial view of the valley. As I drove through the area with my guide, I could see it from the ground level, and I understood why they call it Silicon Valley.

Silicon Valley is located in the southern part of the San Francisco Bay and includes the city of San Jose and the surrounding cities and towns. The "valley" comes from the terrain—it's in the Santa Clara Valley. The "silicon" comes from the large number of silicon chip trailblazers and manufacturers and, more recently, the fact that it's home to the world's largest high-tech corporations. That includes thirty-nine businesses in the Fortune 1000 and thousands of other startup companies. Silicon Valley accounts for one-third of all the venture capital investment in the United States. Because of this, it's developed into a type of venture ecosystem for high-tech innovation and scientific development. It was here that the silicon-based integrated circuit, the microprocessor, and the microcomputer, as well as other key technologies, were developed. As we drove, I saw them—companies that beforehand had been nothing more than a label on a device or a name in an advertisement. And in the middle of a web of expressways and colony of commercial buildings was an impenetrable place of peace and holiness—the shrine of Our Lady of Peace.

The shrine is the only major Marian shrine on the West Coast between Our Lady of Sorrows Shrine in Portland, Oregon (more than 700 miles to the north), and the famous Basilica of Our Lady of Guadalupe in Mexico City, Mexico (more than 2,300 miles to the south). It's part of the parish of Our Lady of Peace, located at the intersection of Freeway 11 and Great America Parkway. The parish was established in 1961 in what was then a rural community, amid acres of orchards and fields. Basically, it was out in the "boondocks," as some described it. In 1969, Msgr. John J. Sweeny became the pastor of Our Lady of Peace and went to work immediately, turning it into a thriving, active parish. In October of that year, he established first friday all-night vigils, and in August 1976, he initiated perpetual adoration. Msgr. Sweeny was exceptionally devoted to our Blessed

Mother and fervently promoted the Rosary to his
parishioners. He wanted them to know the power
of the Rosary and to love Mary as he did.[1]

Msgr. Sweeny had an ambitious dream that
stemmed from his Marian devotion. He wanted to
build a shrine to honor the Immaculate Heart of
Mary on the parish grounds—not just any shrine,
but a magnificent shrine that would speak to her
beauty and importance in the role of salvation
history. It was not only a large dream but also a
costly one, and the parish didn't have the funds
for it. Undaunted, Msgr. Sweeny instructed every
one of his parishioners: "Pray the Rosary and the
money will come." It did—in large donations and
from unexpected places. It was a miracle in the
making. Msgr. Sweeny commissioned the sculptor
Charles C. Parks to build a thirty-two-foot stainless steel statue of our Lady. Parks embraced the
project, working diligently on it in his Wilmington,
Delaware, studio. Because the statue was so large,
he created it outdoors on his lawn. It was such an
oddity that visitors came day and night to observe
the artist at work. Even the mayor of Wilmington
took interest in it as well and, at its completion,
asked Parks to put it on public display in the city's
center. The statue remained there from September
1 to October 10, 1982, and busloads of pilgrims

came from distances to see the statue and to pray there. It gained so much attention that *Delaware Today* magazine published an article with full color pictures titled, "The Madonna Phenomenon."[2] Transporting the statue from Delaware to California caused quite a stir as well. The statue had to be disassembled and loaded onto trucks that formed a caravan and traveled across the United States, stopping in various cities along the way. People would come from miles to see the statue as it passed through their area, and the excitement for it grew.[3]

The statue arrived at Our Lady of Peace Catholic Church in Santa Clara in early October, 1983. A twelve-foot landscaped mound was formed, and on it was placed the 7,200-pound statue. (It was so heavy because the head, hands, and feet were cast in stainless steel and the gown was constructed of welded strips of stainless steel.) The statue still stands there today. Together with the foundation, it rises higher than most three-story buildings and rests at the top of an incline surrounded by a walking path lined with the Stations of the Cross. Mary is just yards away from the front door of the church and looks out over the San Jose Valley.

The statue was dedicated on October 7, 1983—the Feast of Our Lady of the Rosary and, as Msgr.

Sweeny noted, the fifteenth anniversary of the beginning of monthly first Friday all-night vigils in the parish. The bishop of the Diocese of San Jose dedicated the shrine, and Pope John Paul II bestowed a papal blessing for the occasion. For three days that year—October 7 through 9—religious and civic ceremonies and public acknowledgments took place at the foot of the statue. At the final service on Sunday, October 9, Fr. Patrick Peyton, C.S.C., of the Family Rosary Crusade gave the homily. The statue was nicknamed "The Awesome Madonna."[4]

Indeed, she is. I saw her before I saw her shrine. From down the road and above the tops of buildings, I saw our Blessed Mother lovingly beckoning to all who pass by. It's not that the surrounding buildings are so small but rather that she is so, well, *large*. Frankly, I never thought I would like an image of Mary formed in metal, but this one is truly exceptional. It is so exquisitely crafted and she is so beautiful that I immediately fell in love with her. Her expression is what I like most of all: her face is full of love and pleading as she looks out over Highway 101 and across the valley. Her hands are extended not in blessing, as we see in other images, but rather in a gesture of beckoning.

She's calling to her children, "Come. Please come to me."

But there's more. She calls her children to herself not for herself but for her Son. Mary's mission always has been and always will be to lead us to Jesus. She carries on this mission at the shrine of Our Lady of Peace in the most astonishing way. The shrine is also a vibrant Catholic parish with perpetual adoration. You could say that it's the "shrine that never sleeps" because the church and shrine are open 24/7. Anyone, everyone, can go there to visit our Lady and adore her beloved Son at any time of day or night throughout the year.

She calls to her children to come closer to Jesus and experience his presence in the monstrance. And they come. The parish has three Masses daily and the Rosary is prayed communally at the beginning of each hour, led by volunteers. There are ten weekend Masses, and it's common to have upwards of 6,000 people in attendance. Special events can attract an even larger number of attendees. The daily Mass I attended took place in a full church. This, too, was part of Msgr. Sweeny's dream. He wanted the shrine to honor the Immaculate Heart of Mary, and it most certainly does, in an outstanding way. More than that, however, he wanted it done in such a way that Mary would gather people to her Son. Her motherly beauty and love, the welcoming expression on her face, and the beckoning manner in which she extends her hands draw her children in, but they are only able to be drawn in because of what happens around the clock throughout the entire year in the parish church behind her. Msgr. Sweeny knew that Mary's Immaculate Heart would capture hearts that came to adore her Son in his Real Presence, cleanse their souls in the Sacrament of Reconciliation, and receive Jesus in the Eucharist. That, in fact, is the allure of the shrine of Our Lady of Peace. Clearly, our Lady is effective there because the people come, not just in twos and threes, but in dozens, hundreds, even thousands. The parking lot is never empty and the line to the confessional is always steady. To have *three* daily Masses at all, much less Masses that fill the church, is unusual to say the least, especially when so many parishes are limiting the number of their weekday Masses. In every sense of the word, there's more there than meets the eye.

In 2000, Msgr. Sweeny commissioned one last statue for his beloved parish. It's a bronze statue of St. John Paul II and is opposite our Lady on the shrine path. They gaze at each other in love and gratitude. In 2002, Msgr. Sweeny retired as pastor of Our Lady of Peace Catholic Church and passed away not long after. Upon his departure from the parish, the priests of the Institute of the Incarnate Word were enlisted to conduct the parish with the support of their female branch, the Servants of the Lord and the Virgin of Matará. These two religious communities take seriously Msgr. Sweeny's dream and have made his mission their own, tirelessly serving the parish and shrine in every possible capacity. It's through their dedication and direction that the parish continues not only to thrive but also to grow in leaps and bounds with a variety of programs and events added to educate children and support families.

The shrine is aptly named, as well, for the entire place is enveloped in an aura of peace. The peace there is so tangible that you could almost scoop some up to hold in your hands. It seems incredible that all of this takes place right in the middle of the worldly, hectic, ever-changing empire of technology. The contrast is striking, shocking, and miraculous. As I prayed in the church during eucharistic adoration, I could feel the power of Christ drawing the faithful into his Sacred Heart. Holy Mass was the same. That reverence and peace flows out of the church doors and over the land that encompasses the shrine. In

turn, Mary's love for her Divine Son flows from
the shrine and back into the church. The one flows
into the other and vice versa.

I meditated on this as I wandered the
grounds and observed the faithful as they came
to the shrine. They came, stood at Mary's feet, fell
immediately to their knees, and remained there—
motionless—for extended periods of time with
their hands folded and gazing up at her beautiful
face. Parents brought their children and let them
touch her feet and the hem of her gown. Sponta-
neously, they returned Mary's look of love. I went
up and stood at the foot of the statue myself and,
like the others, couldn't help but drop to my knees
and pray there in silence. Then I stood up and cir-
cled the base of the statue, facing outward so that
I could see everything that Mary could see (or at
least everything I could see from my height versus
hers). Peppering the landscape all around were the
logos of major companies that power the world
with their technologies. But the real power was
not in them at all. It was in the tabernacle of the
church just yards from where I stood.

Of all of the shrines I visited during Marian
pilgrimage, the shrine of Our Lady of Peace is the
most modern both in its chronological age and
structure. What might that mean? Hundreds of

years ago, Mary came to this land to claim it for herself and for her Son. She crossed every frontier to carry out her mission, from the shores of the Atlantic, through the Appalachians, over the prairie lands, across the Rocky Mountains, and on to the Pacific Coast. The newest frontier for our nation is not geographic but technological. The territory yet to be claimed and conquered for her Son is knowledge, information, and cyberspace. Mary, with her exquisite and powerful countenance, stands in the center of Silicon Valley in a gesture of welcome, leading all to her Son. But also, I think, with an underlying attitude of defiance. She is serious about her mission, and there is no frontier she will not cross for our sake.

Viewing Our Interior Landscape

We Americans love our gadgets, don't we? We can't wait for the new device to come out that will make our lives easier, help us do things faster, and keep us ahead of everybody else. Consider how customers will wait in long, long lines to get the latest iPhone or the newest smart TV. We want it all and we want it now.

Are you intrigued by gadgets? Do you depend on technology for your entertainment, your information, or your work? If you had to do without your gadgets for a month, could you manage? For a week? For a day? In our present-day times, it is indeed difficult to do completely without technology; it seems that's how the entire world is run. What "runs" your world? How has technology impacted your life? In some ways, technology is a spiritual frontier in that it brings with it an array of temptations that weren't present a generation ago. How are you handling those temptations? Perhaps you need to escape to an oasis such as Our Lady of Peace Shrine, a place where you can encounter our Lord and his Mother and where your soul can be at rest, even if only for short intervals of time. If you are honest with yourself, you'll see that you need time and space to find peace and to be alone with our Lord. Ask Our Lady of Peace to help you discover that oasis. Then go there and rest in her motherly heart.

The Journey Begins

Offer yourself, your loved ones, and our country to Mary, asking her intercession that a profound longing for Christ may fill your heart and the hearts of all the people of the United States. Then consecrate yourself and our nation to the Blessed Virigin Mary.

My Queen, My Mother,

I give myself entirely to you. And to show my devotion to you, I consecrate to you this day, my eyes, my ears, my mouth, my heart, my entire self without reserve. As I am your own, my good Mother, guard me and defend me as your property and possession. Amen.

Pray the Rosary for those who struggle with addictions to technology that they may be healed of their addiction and pursue endeavors that will lead themselves and others to Jesus and his holy Mother. Pray also for the leaders of our country that they may guide our nation with wisdom and godly principles.

Stepping Out in Faith

- What most impresses you about the story of the shrine of Our Lady of Peace?

- What "frontiers" are in you that our Blessed Mother must yet conquer? How can you open yourself to her so that she can conquer each one?

- What is your dream—for yourself, your family, and our country? How can you ensure that it rests in God's providence?

Conclusion

I have only one regret about my pilgrimage: I regret that I couldn't include more shrines! There are so many astonishing Marian places of grace across the United States, that I could travel non-stop for years and not have seen them all! I wish I could. On the other hand, I don't think that's what our Blessed Mother had in mind when she put the idea for the project on my heart. You see, *I'm* not the one who is meant to visit all the sites that honor Mary; *you are.* What I've done here (hopefully, and by the grace of God) is to whet your appetite so that you strike out on your own to see what Marian shrines, churches, basilicas, cathedrals, missions, or grottos you can discover in your own area and beyond. With each place you visit, you'll learn more about Mary and fall more deeply in love with her as your heavenly Mother. What's more, you'll discover more about this great nation of ours and all that it has to offer despite any drawbacks it might have. This wonderful country is *our* wonderful country, and we must affirm our love for it and stand firm in godly unity for its posterity.

It's tragic that large numbers of Marian pilgrimage places are little known and rarely visited.

It's a shame that often they must cut budgets and reduce hours of operation for lack of funding and people to run them. There's a beautiful history behind every one of them, and Mary has chosen a special title and mission for herself at each site. She'll continue her presence and mission for as long as she's welcome, and it's up to us to extend that welcome. Through this book, we have consecrated ourselves and our country to Mary. By continuing to visit the precious yet often obscure Marian sites that grace the regions of the United States, we'll continue to live that consecration and secure it for future generations. Our visits must be repeated and expanded; our consecration must be renewed and multiplied.

Our US heritage is inexhaustibly rich and our Catholic heritage within it is even more so. Mary has come to claim and conquer the United States for her Son and she wants you, me—all of us—to do the same.

Appendix

HOW TO PRAY THE ROSARY

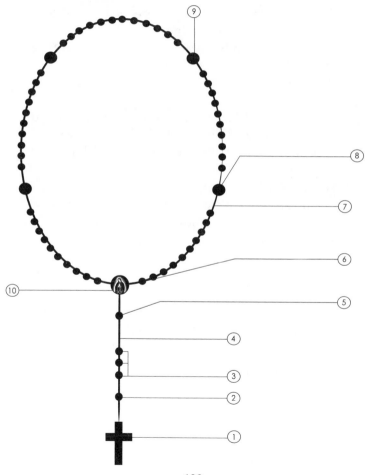

1. Make the Sign of the Cross and say the Apostles' Creed.
2. On the first large bead, say the Our Father.
3. On the next three small beads, say a Hail Mary.
4. Say the Glory Be.
5. On the next large bead, announce the first mystery, and then say the Our Father.
6. On each of the next nine small beads, say a Hail Mary while meditating on that mystery.
7. On the tenth bead, say a Hail Mary followed by a Glory Be.
8. On the second large bead announce the second mystery, followed by the Our Father.
9. Repeat steps 6–7. Continue with the third through fifth mysteries in the same manner.
10. When you have completed the prayers for all five mysteries, conclude with a Hail, Holy Queen and Fatima Prayer, followed by the Prayer to St. Michael. Then make the Sign of the Cross.

The Mysteries of the Rosary

The mysteries of the Rosary commemorate key events in the life of Christ and the Blessed Mother; by meditating upon these mysteries we grow in faith, hope, and love. (For more information about each mystery, go to www.rosary-center.org/howto. htm#loaded.)

The Joyful Mysteries (Monday, Saturday): The Annunciation, the Visitation, the Nativity, the Presentation, the Finding of Jesus in the Temple

The Sorrowful Mysteries (Tuesday, Friday): The Agony in the Garden, the Scourging at the Pillar, the Crowning with Thorns, the Carrying of the Cross, the Crucifixion

The Luminous Mysteries (Thursday): The Baptism of the Lord, the Wedding at Cana, the Proclamation of the Kingdom, the Transfiguration, the Institution of the Eucharist

The Glorious Mysteries (Wednesday, Sunday): The Resurrection, the Ascension, the Descent of the Holy Spirit, the Assumption, the Coronation of Mary as Queen of Heaven

The Prayers of the Rosary

THE APOSTLES' CREED

I believe in God, the Father almighty, Creator of heaven and earth, and in Jesus Christ, his only Son, our Lord, who was conceived by the Holy Spirit, born of the Virgin Mary, suffered under Pontius Pilate, was crucified, died, and was buried; he descended into hell; on the third day he rose again from the dead; he ascended into heaven, and is seated at the right hand of God, the Father

Almighty; from there he will come to judge the living and the dead. I believe in the Holy Spirit, the holy catholic Church, the Communion of Saints, the forgiveness of sins, the resurrection of the body and life everlasting. Amen.

THE OUR FATHER

Our Father, who art in heaven, hallowed be thy name. Thy kingdom come; thy will be done on earth as it is in heaven. Give us this day our daily bread and forgive us our trespasses as we forgive those who trespass against us. And lead us not into temptation, but deliver us from evil. Amen.

THE HAIL MARY

Hail Mary, full of grace, the Lord is with thee. Blessed art thou among women and blessed is the fruit of thy womb, Jesus. Holy Mary, Mother of God, pray for us sinners now and at the hour of our death. Amen.

THE GLORY BE

Glory be to the Father and to the Son and to the Holy Spirit, as it was in the beginning, is now, and ever shall be, world without end. Amen.

HAIL, HOLY QUEEN

Hail, holy Queen, Mother of Mercy, our life, our sweetness and our hope! To thee do we cry, poor banished children of Eve. To thee do we send up our sighs, mourning and weeping in this valley of tears. Turn then, most gracious advocate, thine eyes of mercy toward us, and after this our exile, show unto us the blessed fruit of thy womb, Jesus. O clement, O loving, O sweet Virgin Mary!

> V. Pray for us, O Holy Mother of God.
> R. That we may be made worthy of the promises of Christ.

Let us pray: O God, whose Only Begotten Son, by his life, Death, and Resurrection, has purchased for us the rewards of eternal life, grant, we beseech thee, that while meditating on these mysteries of the most holy Rosary of the Blessed Virgin Mary, we may imitate what they contain and obtain what they promise, through the same Christ Our Lord. Amen.

FATIMA PRAYER

O my Jesus, forgive us our sins, save us from the fires of hell; lead all souls to heaven, especially those who have most need of your mercy.

PRAYER TO ST. MICHAEL

Saint Michael the Archangel, defend us in battle. Be our protection against the wickedness and snares of the devil. May God rebuke him, we humbly pray. And do thou, o prince of the heavenly host—by the divine power of God—cast into hell Satan and all the evil spirits, who roam throughout the world seeking the ruin of souls. Amen.

Notes

INTRODUCTION

1. Eleonore Villarrubia, "Catholic Pilgrimage, A Spiritual Journey," Catholicism.org, July 17, 2010, http://catholicism.org/catholic-pilgrimage-a-spiritual-journey.html.

2. Villarubia, "Catholic Pilgrimage."

3. Benedict XVI, Visit to the Cathedral of Santiago de Compostela, November 6, 2010, https://w2.vatican.va/content/benedict-xvi/en/speeches/2010/november/documents/hf_ben-xvi_spe_20101106_cattedrale-compostela.html.

DAY ONE

1. Our Lady of La Leche Shrine, exhibition documentation examined by the author, April 25, 2018.

2. Our Lady of La Leche Shrine, exhibition documentation.

3. John McKeown (historian, Shrine of Our Lady of La Leche), interview with the author, April 25, 2018.

DAY TWO

1. Mary Lee Harris (historian, Shrine of Our Lady of Prompt Succor), interview with the author, April 27, 2018.

2. Harris, interview.

3. Harris, interview.

4. Old Ursuline Convent Museum archives, Letter of Thomas Jefferson to Sr. Therese de S' Xavier Fajon, May 15, 1804, Old Ursuline Convent Museum.

5. Old Ursuline Convent Museum archives.

6. Harris, interview.

7. Harris, interview.

DAY THREE

1. Anne. W. Carroll, *Christ and the Americas* (Charlotte, NC: Tan Books, 1997), 176.

2. St. Mary's Mission and Museum, exhibition documentation examined by the author, May 16, 2018.

3. St. Mary's Mission and Museum, exhibition documentation.

4. Colleen Meyer (historian, St. Mary's Mission and Museum), interview with the author and examination of documentation, May 16, 2018.

5. Meyer, interview.

6. Meyer, interview and documentation.

7. Lucylle H. Evans, *St. Mary's in the Rocky Mountains: A History of the Cradle of Montana Culture* (Stevensville, Montana: Montana Creative Consultants, 1976), 107–123.

8. Evans, 149–151.

9. "History of St. Mary's Mission," Historic St. Mary's Mission and Museum, accessed May 25, 2018, http://www.saintmarysmission.org/history.

10. Evans, 201–210.

11. Evans, 215–221.

12. Evans, 51.

13. Pierre Jean DeSmet, *Origin, Progress, and Prospects of the Catholic Mission to the Rocky Mountains* (Ye Galleon Press Fairfield, Washington, 1986), 7–9.

DAY FOUR

1. "US Immigration Trends 1800s," accessed May 25, 2018, http://www.emmigration.info/us-immigration-trends-early-1800%27s.htm.

2. "The Beginning of St. Martin's Church and the Shrine of Our Lady of Sorrows," Shrine of Our Lady of Sorrows, Starkenburg, Missouri, accessed May 25, 2018, http://vivaro-hshrine-primary.cluster2.hgsitebuilder.com/history.

3. Shirley Koenig (historian, Shrine of Our Lady of Sorrows), interview with the author, October 11, 2018.

4. "The Beginning of St. Martin's Church and the Shrine of Our Lady of Sorrows," The Shrine of Our Lady of Sorrows, Starkenburg, Missouri, accessed May 25, 2018, http:// vivaro-hshrine-primary.cluster2.hgsitebuilder.com/history.

5. Koenig, interview.

6. "The Beginning of St. Martin's Church and the Shrine of Our Lady of Sorrows."

7. Koenig, interview.

8. Koenig, interview.

DAY FIVE

1. "Timeline of Discovery," Harvard Medical School, accessed August 31, 2018, https://hms.harvard.edu/ about-hms/history-hms/timeline-discovery.

2. "Milestones in Medical Discovery," *New York Times*, October 10, 2012, https://archive.nytimes.com/www. nytimes.com/interactive/2012/10/05/health/digital-doc-tor.html?ref=thedigitaldoctor#/#time15_371.

3. "Timeline of Discovery."

4. "Timeline of Discovery."

5. "Timeline of Discovery."

6. "About Carey, Ohio," The Progressor Times.com, accessed August 31, 2018, https://www.theprogressortimes. com/carey-history.

7. Jeffrey Hines, O.F.M. Conv., *Our Lady of Consolation: A History of the Basilica and National Shrine* (Carey, OH: Basilica and National Shrine of Our Lady of Consolation, 2012), 4.

8. Hines, *Our Lady of Consolation*, 5–11.

9. Hines, *Our Lady of Consolation*, 5–11.

10. Hines, *Our Lady of Consolation*, 5–11.

11. Hines, *Our Lady of Consolation*, 5–11.

12. Hines, *Our Lady of Consolation*, 10.

13. Hines, *Our Lady of Consolation*, 18.

14. Hines, *Our Lady of Consolation*, 15.

15. Hines, *Our Lady of Consolation*, 9.

16. *Basilica of Our Lady of Consolation Walking Tour* (Carey, OH: Basilica and National Shrine of Our Lady of Consolation), exhibition brochure.

17. *Basilica of Our Lady of Consolation Walking Tour*, exhibition brochure.

DAY SIX

1. "Spiritual Tourism in France on the Rise," Tourism Review, April 24, 2017, https://tourism-review.com/spiritual-tourism-lures-tourists-to-france-news5374.

2. "Religious Tourism in Portugal Booming," Tourism Review, May 8, 2017, https://www.tourism-review.com/religious-tourism-in-portugal-growing-news5394.

3. Adele's last name is also spelled "Brise," and both forms are used at the shrine.

4. M. Dominica, O.S.F., "The Chapel of Our Lady of Good Help" (Green Bay, WI: Sisters of St. Francis of Bay Settlement, 1955), 5.

5. Dominica, "The Chapel of Our Lady of Good Help," 7.

6. Dominica, "The Chapel of Our Lady of Good Help," 8–9.

7. Corrie Campbell (historian, The National Shrine of Our Lady of Good Help), interview with the author, June 23, 2017.

8. Dominica, "The Chapel of Our Lady of Good Help," 14.

9. The National Shrine of Our Lady of Good Help, exhibition documentation examined by the author, June 23, 2017.

10. Campbell, interview.

11. Kim Estep, "The Peshtigo Fire," *Green Bay Press-Gazette*, as quoted on National Weather Service, accessed June 7, 2018, https://www.weather.gov/grb/peshtigofire.

12. Campbell, interview.

13. Dominica, "The Chapel of Our Lady of Good Help," 26–41.

14. Campbell, interview.

DAY SEVEN

1. Beth Lynch (executive director and historian, Shrine of Our Lady of Martyrs), interview with the author, October 23, 2017.

2. Timothy E. Byerly, *The Great Commission: Models of Evangelization in American Catholicism* (New York: Paulist Press, 2008), 18–19.

3. Byerly, 17.

4. Shrine of Our Lady of Martyrs, exhibition documentation examined by the author, October 23, 2017.

5. Shrine of Our Lady of Martyrs, exhibition documentation.

6. Lynch, interview.

7. Lynch, interview.

8. Lynch, interview.

9. Lynch, interview.

10. Lynch, interview.

DAY EIGHT

1. Robert H. Bremner, *American Philanthropy* (Chicago: University of Chicago Press, 1987), 5–6.

2. Karl Zinsmeister, *The Almanac of American Philanthropy: 2017*, Compact Edition (Washington, DC: The Philanthropy Roundtable, 2017), 350.

3. Zinsmeister, 1689.

4. Jean Weller (historian, the House of Mary Shrine), interview with the author, May 4, 2018.

5. Weller, interview.

6. The House of Mary Shrine, exhibition documentation examined by the author, May 4, 2018.

DAY NINE

1. Karen Ruiz (historian, Shrine of Our Lady of Peace), interviewed by the author, February 21, 2018.

2. Shrine of Our Lady of Peace, exhibition documentation examined by the author, February 21, 2018.

3. Accounts relayed to author via email and social media messaging.

4. Shrine of Our Lady of Peace, exhibition documentation.

Marge Steinhage Fenelon is a bestselling Catholic author, award-winning journalist, and popular speaker. She blogs regularly at *National Catholic Register* and is a columnist for the *Milwaukee Catholic Herald*. Fenelon has appeared on EWTN and is a frequent guest on many Catholic radio shows nationwide. She is the author of several books on Marian devotion and Catholic spirituality, including *Imitating Mary* and the award-winning *Our Lady, Undoer of Knots*.

Fenelon is an instructor for the Archdiocese of Milwaukee Deacon Wives' Program and, along with her husband, Mark, is a consecrated member of the Apostolic Movement of Schoenstatt. The Fenelons live in Milwaukee, Wisconsin.

www.margefenelon.com
Facebook: @margesteinhagefenelon
Twitter: @MargeSteinFen

ALSO BY
MARGE STEINHAGE FENELON

Our Lady, Undoer of Knots: A Living Novena is a unique guided meditation from veteran Catholic journalist Marge Steinhage Fenelon, who has created a new devotional practice from this classic novena that is a favorite of Pope Francis.

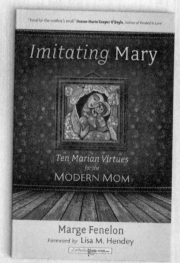

In an age when women are bombarded with mothering advice, Marge Steinhage Fenelon delves into ten instances—and corresponding virtues—of Mary's life that reveal her as the ultimate model and companion for the modern mom.